The Church for Disciples of Christ

The Church for Disciples of Christ

Seeking to be Truly Church Today

by Commission on Theology
Christian Church (Disciples of Christ)
Originally Edited by
Paul A. Crow, Jr. and James O. Duke
1998

Reissued 2008
Edited by Robert K. Welsh, President
Council on Christian Unity
Christian Church (Disciples of Christ)
P.O. Box 1986, Indianapolis, Indiana 46206

ST. LOUIS, MISSOURI

ISBN: 978-1-603500-04-3

Published by Lucas Park Books
www.lucasparkbooks.com

Printed in the United States of America

Contents

PREFACE

An Invitation to Conversation

Disciples of Christ often have quoted the phrase, "In essentials unity, in opinions liberty, and in all things charity"—a verse not original with us—as one of those slogans that mark our identity as a movement and as a church. Sounds easy. But, the problem continues to reside in agreeing on what are "essentials" and what are "opinions."

It was the stated task of our church's Commission on Theology to sort out the "essentials" of what it means to be the Disciples of Christ that gave rise to the material included in this volume. As stated in the volume originally published in 1998, edited by Paul A. Crow, Jr. and James O. Duke, "In this report the Commission on Theology of the Council on Christian Unity seeks to answer the most basic and all-embracing question facing the Christian Church (Disciples of Christ) today: what do Disciples think it means to be church?"

For over 20 years (1979-1997) that Commission contributed biennial reports as *"A Word to the Church"* on what Disciples believe about the nature of the church, its witness, mission and unity, plus the questions of authority, ministry, baptism, and the Lord's Supper.

This volume is a reissue of this material, **The Church for Disciples of Christ: Seeking to be Truly Church Today**, which sets forth a context of what "being church" is all about [Part 1: *"Seeking to Be Truly the Church;"* Part 2: *"Lessons from Scripture and Tradition;"* Part 3: *"The Defining Signs of the Church's Identity;"* Part 4: *"Issues of Relationship and Structure;"* and, Part 5: the reports of the Theology Commission to the General Assembly of the Christian Church (Disciples of Christ).]

The beauty of "church" as experienced among the Disciples of Christ is that doing theology is not the domain solely of a "theology commission" but involves the whole church in all its expressions. That is why the reissue of this small volume becomes important. The Commission encourages clergy and laity alike to wrestle with the questions raised herein in local settings and discussions.

For instance, the Theology Commission in 1991 said the Lord's Supper, which Disciples quickly recognize as central to their worship, preferably should come at the end of the worship service. Is that true in your congregation? Further, what is the role and relationship of the ordained minister to the elders at the Table? Is it appropriate for unbaptized children to take communion? See what the theology commission has to say about those matters.

And what about authority in the church? How does the church teach with authority? When, and under what circumstances, does the church speak with authority? The commission says Christ is always persuasive, never coercive. Among Disciples, authority is dispersed and shared, says the Commission. How does that play out in church life?

Since the whole people of God are called to share in mission, what are the appropriate involvements of the church in the struggle for justice and liberation? How do lay people minister to one another? Where is God calling us as Disciples today in mission and ministry?

It is my hope that this volume will spark renewed and fresh discussion across the life of our church, regarding the "essentials" of what it means to be church today! Only then will the tradition of theologizing among the rank and file of Disciples be perpetuated.

Those who served on the Commission represent some of the leading theologians of the Disciples tradition (*listed below*). Across the years the Commission was led by two chairpersons—H. Jackson Forstman (Vanderbilt University Divinity School) and James O. Duke (Brite Divinity School) – and guided by the vision of Paul A. Crow, Jr., my predecessor as Ecumenical Officer for the Christian Church (Disciples of Christ).

— Robert Welsh, president of the Council on Christian Unity

Commission on Theology (1997)

Members

Paul A. Crow, Jr.
President, Council on Christian Unity
Indianapolis, Indiana

Kristine Culp
Disciples Divinity House
Chicago, Illinois

Richard L. Harrison, Jr.
Lexington Theological Seminary
Lexington, Kentucky

Kenneth Henry
Interdenominational Theological Center
Atlanta, Georgia

William Tabbernee
Phillips Theological Seminary
Tulsa, Oklahoma

James O. Duke
Brite Divinity School
Ft. Worth, Texas

H. Jackson Forstman
Vanderbilt Divinity School
Nashville, Tennessee

Michael Kinnamon
Lexington Theological Seminary
Lexington, Kentucky

Joe R. Jones
Christian Theological Seminary
Indianapolis, Indiana

Consultants

Richard L. Hamm
General Minister and President
Christian Church (Disciples of Christ)

Carmelo Alvarez
Christian Theological Seminary
Indianapolis, Indiana

Linda Patrick-Rosebrock
Augusta Christian Church
Indianapolis, Indiana

PREAMBLE

The Identity of the Community Called to Be Church

The church is that community called into being by the Gospel, which is God's covenant of love in Jesus Christ, and given its life through the power of God's Spirit in order to praise and serve the living God. All those who accept this calling—of whatever race, nationality, or culture—are joined together as one people commissioned by God to witness by word and deed to God's love for the world. They signify their corporate identity by:

- their common confession of faith that Jesus is the Christ, the Son of the living God,
- their incorporation into the body of Christ through baptism,
- their thankful celebration of Christ's saving work and abiding presence through the Lord's Supper,
- their common commitment to direct their lives in accord with the will of God as made known through the testimony of Scripture, and
- their shared experience of the Holy Spirit who empowers them for ministry as disciples and ambassadors of Christ to and for the world.

This community, through its life of unity in diversity as well as its witness in word and deed, exists to glorify God, proclaiming from generation to generation and to the ends of the earth God's good news in Jesus Christ, participating in God's work of reconciliation, liberation, and redemption for all people, and thus living as a sign of God's coming reign.

This statement seeks to describe the identity of the community called forth by God to be the one, Universal

Church of Jesus Christ. It focuses on the essentials which unite all those who participate in this church and which distinguish this community from every other in the world. It is drawn from Scripture, ecumenical dialogue, and the particular experience of the community of faith known as Disciples of Christ.

The statement gives rise to affirmations and questions worthy of careful consideration by members of the Christian Church (Disciples of Christ).

1. The church is first and foremost a gift of God. Is it not then a misunderstanding to think of the church as no more than the product of a human urge for fellowship?
2. The church is essentially a community formed by its members' relationship to Christ and thus to one another. Is it not then a misunderstanding to think of the church only in terms of the buildings in which the community gathers?
3. The church is a community whose life together—as one people—is essential to its character as a sign of God's reconciling purpose for all creation. Is it not then a misunderstanding to think of the church as a loose-knit association of individuals or coalition of groups?
4. The church exists for the sake of praising God and participating in God's mission in and for all the world. Is it not then a misunderstanding to think that the church's sole or primary purpose is to satisfy the needs and desires of its own members?
5. The church's unity is founded, and utterly dependent, on the reconciling love of God in Christ. Is it not then a misunderstanding to think that the unity of the church is formed simply by human agreement and so may be broken simply because of human disagreement?
6. The church witnesses to God's intended wholeness for all creation by transcending in its own life those barriers of race, sex, culture, class, and nationality that divide persons from one another. Is it not then a misunderstanding to think that the church may exclude

any of the God-given diversity of the human family or limit leadership in the church on the basis of race, gender, culture, class, or national background?

7. The church is a universal fellowship that "appears wherever believers in Jesus Christ are gathered in his name" (*Design*, ¶2). Is it not then a misunderstanding to think of the church only as a local congregation of believers?
8. The church must develop an organizational structure in order to fulfill its God-given mission, but no one form of organization is essential to its true identity because the church "in faithfulness to its mission…continues to adapt its structure to the needs and patterns of a changing world" (*Design*, ¶2). Is it not then a misunderstanding to think that any particular structure of the church is ordained by God for all times and all places?
9. The covenant on which the church is founded is initiated and sealed by God. Is it not then a misunderstanding to think of the church's covenantal bonds of love solely in terms of contractual obligations toward present organizational structures?
10. The church extends across time as well as space, binding together all who confess Jesus Christ in whatever age. Is it not then a misunderstanding to think that we may make the church what we will, without regard for the witness of the faithful who have come before us and for our obligations to the faithful who are to come after us?
11. Membership in the church is a matter of humble gratitude to God and joyful responsibility rather than a privilege and has nothing to do with human merit. Is it not then a misunderstanding to think that belonging to the church is a cause for boasting of special status before God?
12. The chief end of the church, like that of life itself, is to glorify God. Is it not then a misunderstanding to think of the church as an arena for human aggrandizement?

PART 1

Seeking to Be Truly Church

Faithfulness calls Christians in every age to examine our understanding of the church's identity. By this means the church seeks to refresh its awareness of its God-given nature and purpose and so to live in more perfect accord with the will of God. This task falls to Disciples at the end of the twentieth century as it has to each preceding generation.

The preamble entitled "The Identity of the Community Called to be Church" is the result of study and reflection on the meaning of the church for the Disciples carried out by the Theology Commission of the Council on Christian Unity of the Christian Church (Disciples of Christ).* All that follows in this report is in one sense commentary on the preamble. It is also—in another, larger sense—an open invitation to all Disciples to join the Commission in its work by retracing, reviewing, adding to, and improving upon the account offered here. This report is therefore designed not only to record the Commission's thoughts about the church but to aid others in their own efforts to understand the identity, nature, and purpose of the church more clearly and fully.

Toward Understanding the Identity of the Church

Questions about the nature of Christian community and church life arise all the time. For example, when Disciples speak of Christian unity, what kind of unity do we envision? Why bother to work and pray for the oneness of the church when the effort seems so unpopular, untimely, or unproductive? Should Disciples stay together in fellowship even when we disagree on issues of faith? Which matters are "essentials" and which are "non-essentials" in the Christian life? How can we attend to the diversity of voices in the church and still proclaim the one Gospel with clarity and boldness? Is mission something the local church does or something we support others to do in our name? If it is both, where is the priority? Granted that regional ministers are more than administrators and regional offices more than consultative agencies, how are we to understand their roles in our church overall? Is it ever proper for congregations to develop along distinctive racial-ethnic or cultural lines, and if so, when, where, and why? Should Disciples pay any attention to the witness of the church in the past, and is that witness in any sense authoritative for us today? How are Disciples to discern the common mind of the church when we disagree about matters of belief, personal morality, or social issues? When asked if Disciples permit people to repeat their baptism or invite young, unbaptized children to the Lord's Table, what are we prepared to say about the meaning of baptism and the Lord's Supper? How should Disciples view our relationship to Christians in other parts of the world and make that relationship real?

These, and countless others we could name, are questions of *ecclesiology*. This is to say that they have to do with our understanding of the identity, nature, and purpose of the church (the *ecclesia*, "assembly"). Our answers as well as our silences to such questions disclose something about our understanding of the church. Each of us already carries some understanding of church—*our* understanding of church—even if we have never tried to state it in just so many words. Such common but pressing questions about the church prompt us to express at least bits and pieces of our ecclesiology.

We disclose much about our understanding of the church simply in the course of taking part in its life and work. Joining and participating in the church surely indicate our understanding that faith in Christ draws us out of isolation and into community and express the importance of the church—certainly for us the particular church to which we belong—for living out this faith. Even without explicitly saying so, we show by our actions that we understand the church to be where Christian faith is awakened, shared, nourished, guided, and expressed in manifold ways. This is, after all, *why* we join and participate in the church, isn't it?

The church is the community in which Christian faith is awakened, shared, nourished, guided, and expressed.

Maybe it would be more accurate to say we understand that all this (and surely more) is what the church is *supposed* to be, what it *ought* to be, what it is *called* to be. The church is called by God to be the community in which Christian faith is awakened, shared, nourished, guided, and expressed in manifold ways. A church that fails to live, to speak, and to act as it should is a church that falls short of its calling. It is not altogether what it is *truly* called to be by God, and therefore somehow something less or other than *truly* church.

What then of the Christian Church (Disciples of Christ): is it *truly* church? This is a question of faith, and one with important practical consequences. Faithfulness calls us to examine our understanding of the church, our ecclesiology, with care. How should we understand what God is calling the church to be?

As persons called together by the beckoning grace of God and members of the Christian Church (Disciples of Christ) at the dawn of the twenty-first century, it falls now to us to give an account of our best understanding of the identity, nature, and purpose of the church. On this basis we are to determine in which respects and to what extent the Christian Church (Disciples of Christ) to which we belong is truly church, part of the universal Church of Jesus Christ. At the outset, we recognize that our understanding of the church is already, and inevitably, shaped by both our own church's heritage and its contemporary situation. We take these influences seriously. But, God willing, we are not so bound by them that we are unable perhaps to see some things more clearly than our forbears did, to recover valuable old resources hitherto overlooked or set aside, and to envision new possibilities for our church in God's future. Thus our heritage and our current situation deserve at least a brief review.

The Church for Disciples Past

Throughout their history, Disciples have sought to discern the true identity of the church by searching the testimony of the Scriptures, especially the New Testament, in light of the best resources available to them and in response to changing situations of opportunity and peril. Three dominant conceptions of church followed one another over the course of time: Church as Citizens of the Kingdom, the Brotherhood, and Covenant Community.

Each conception is based on a prominent biblical theme—the reign of God, fellowship, and covenant. Around each leading theme, many others cluster to form a more richly and fully textured view of the biblical record. The polity (the organizational structure) of our church has been adapted in keeping with these themes and the church's desire to remain faithful to its God-given calling. Our history also reveals that these efforts to understand the identity, nature, and purpose of the church were inevitably shaped by situations and values common in the times.

Citizens of the Kingdom. The conception of church as citizens of the Kingdom came to prominence in the era of our church's origins. The movement led by Barton Warren Stone and Thomas and Alexander Campbell arose in an age when people of the United States celebrated citizenship in a new nation of independence, equality, and self-government. There was also great fear of a return to tyranny, resistance to any attempt to restrict the freedoms of individuals or groups, and impatience with claims of special rank and airs of superiority. What it meant to be a free citizen in a free nation was a topic of constant discussion.

The separation of church and state in the Republic broke the hold of once established churches. One result was the proliferation of churches, old and new, each claiming to be the one true church of Jesus Christ. The situation raised serious questions of faith: How is the true church to be recognized? and What does it mean to belong to that church? The early Disciples relied on the New Testament as the primary authority for answers to these and other issues of faith.

They read the New Testament with care, but also with the eyes of those thankful for newly won freedom, wary of authoritarianism, and confident of their impartiality and accuracy. They discovered in their reading what they perceived to be the few and simple essentials of the church of the apostles, in effect the "original" design of the church. To them, it followed that no power on earth, not even established churches, could rightly deny earnest disciples of Christ their right to form congregations in strict conformity to this design. And they were certain that every church would—or should—agree to require the biblical essentials alone as a test of church fellowship and precondition for Christian unity. In short, at the heart the "Nineteenth Century Reformation" led by Stone and the Campbells was a vision of the church's true identity.

Their conception of church as "citizens of the Kingdom" permitted Disciples to hold several ideas together. Foremost was the New Testament witness to the fulfillment of God's intended purpose for the world, as stated in political imagery—the government, kingdom or reign of God. Alexander Campbell described the church as a constitutional monarchy, with Jesus Christ as the King, and Christians as the "naturalized citizens" of the realm. The Kingdom was founded by the life, death, resurrection, and ascension of Christ, and inaugurated through the sending of the Holy Spirit on Pentecost. To become a citizen of this Kingdom requires an oath of allegiance and a formal ceremony of naturalization. The oath is "the Good Confession." The formal ceremony is baptism (by immersion), a symbolic act of union with God in Christ which, performed by the Kingdom-Church, signifies giving up of (dying to) citizenship in this world and entering into (rebirth) new life by the remission of sins.

Local congregations are settlements or outposts of God's Kingdom. Taken together they form a great community of communities—"one congregation, one mystical or spiritual body." Its citizens live under a common constitution, a "system of grace," which God ordains for the well-being of the whole body. Citizens witness to the unity of faith in corporate worship on Sunday, the Lord's Day. Here they read and proclaim biblical testimony to the Good News of God's unfailing love, and offer up thanks and praise. Their worship reaches its climax with the celebration of the Lord's Supper, when all join with their Savior in table fellowship. In these ways, this immigrant community—of varied racial-ethnic, national, and cultural backgrounds—participates in a reality which extends from the throne of God and the cross of Jesus to the local place of worship, around the globe, and throughout the ages.

Early Disciples saw in the New Testament numerous self-governing congregations that faced little if any restraint from other Christians beyond the local community, and they formed their churches on this model. In some cases, decisions were made by general consent or majority rule. In most cases, voting members elected—and, in regular order, ordained—several leaders (elders or bishops, along with deacons) to exercise representative authority over congregational life. This form of church organization was, they held, in strict accord with biblical precedent and in keeping with their experience of political life generally. Typically, only white male members had voice and vote, as in society at large.

The early Disciples found that they could not do all they should as the Kingdom of God in utter isolation from each other. Cooperation was necessary for congregations to get their start, to survive in times of need, and to minister effectively. Conflict arose over the question of whether any other form of organized church body was permissible and if so, how it should relate to local congregations. Yet it became increasingly evident that evangelism, education for ministry, and even decisions about ordination required a broader vision than that of one, isolated congregation. And as their vision of ministry began to expand beyond their own localities, many came to the realization that just as no one individual can be a Christian in isolation from others, so too no one congregation could be a church—or the Kingdom—all by itself.

Their New Testament model of the church specified only essentials. It left many matters to human discretion, to "expedient" means for furthering the ministry of the church. Frontier-style pragmatism—"if it works, it has value"—did the same. And thus Disciples began to organize, first in regional conferences or associations, then in state meetings. National and even international assemblies soon followed, as Disciples from the United States and Canada gathered together to promote outreach programs—evangelism, medical care, and education—near and far.

Their historical context made early Disciples sensitive to aspects of biblical faith which enabled them to challenge prevailing traditions and to witness to Christ with fervor. It also limited their vision in certain other respects. It is a painful fact that even as the new nation praised liberty, equality, and representative democracy, most African Americans were kept in slave bondage and counted as only three-fifths of a person in census tallies for congressional districts. Disciples recognized that God welcomed people of every race and from every land into the Kingdom, and many of those disenfranchised and otherwise disadvantaged in the American Republic accepted God's invitation and served as faithful followers of Christ and as co-workers in his church. Nonetheless, our church's record on the issue of slavery and its treatment of African Americans rarely differed from patterns set by society generally. Likewise, stereotypes and discriminatory attitudes common to the time relegated women to second-class citizenship in the church.

The Brotherhood. From the middle years of the nineteenth century, Disciples made a shift in their understanding of church that would guide them for almost a century. More and more they began to speak of themselves as "the Brotherhood." A key element in the new model was its emphasis on the personality, life, and teachings of Jesus, which brought with it a more expansive understanding of discipleship. Although unwavering in the conviction that local congregations were truly church, they could no longer rest content to think that these alone could perform the many and varied ministries to which disciples of Christ were called by their Master. Just as Jesus served others, so his disciples are called to serve them—to address the great needs and spiritual longings of people both near and far. Christ's disciples fulfill their calling by following his teachings and life example. The church itself is only the first stage of the coming Kingdom. Christians must work together to complete its upbuilding on earth. In all this, the church marches forward—not necessarily in lockstep with the strict letter of apostolic law but imbued with the selfless spirit of Jesus and inspired by the high ideals with which the apostles set out to "win the world for Christ." The call to build up the Kingdom motivated brothers and sisters in Christ to develop a vast network of cooperative organizations for wider service at home and abroad, including ecumenical ventures, and led Disciples to reconsider their corporate identity.

Our church's record on slavery and its treatment of African Americans rarely differed from patterns set by society.

The concept of "Brotherhood" struck a deep and responsive chord among many Disciples. Congregational independence, now joined with an emphasis on warm fellowship with the Savior and his followers and a grand vision of worldwide ministry, contributed to remarkable overall growth during this era. Yet there were troubling issues to be faced. Some were by now no longer new. Those Disciples who were among America's racial minorities—

African Americans constituting the largest number in this day—made invaluable contributions to the church's witness. Even so, opportunities to experience a sense of genuine "brotherhood" were rarely afforded them by their European-American co-workers. Female Disciples, who often pioneered "Brotherhood work," nevertheless had to struggle to have their leadership recognized within the whole church. Indeed, the term "Brotherhood" itself in effect passed them over.

Other issues were new. The character of the Brotherhood as a way of being church left much to be desired. So many program agencies and institutions were formed that all of them were hard-pressed to gain adequate backing. "Brotherly" cooperation often gave way to duplication of effort and unhealthy competition. Stormy, often bitter, arguments broke out over the biblical justification for many—or even any—of the "innovations" of the day, and so too over how to interpret the Scriptures responsibly. Cooperation or non-cooperation in Brotherhood organizations and causes became in effect a test of fellowship. The "family" suffered two break-ups during the period from 1865 to the 1920s.

Covenant Community. Twentieth-century Disciples have attempted a series of organizational adjustments—realignment, downsizing, expansion, consolidation. Advances on one front were frequently matched by reversals on another. The need to bring order out of chaos and at the same time embody the reality of the wholeness of church led them at mid-century to reappraise their understanding of the church. New language—language in fact as old as the faith of ancient Israel, and on occasion cited by our church's founders—came into frequent use. To be church, it was said in Disciples circles, is to be a community in covenant with God and with one another. The biblical accounts of covenanting tell of more than working side-by-side in a more or less cooperative fashion. A covenant is a vow, a solemn pledge, of loyalty among two or more parties. Entering into covenant with God and with one another means that we have sacred promises to keep: promises of unfailing dedication to a common mission, promises of mutual support, care, and accountability, promises of fidelity.

The conception of church as covenant community came to institutional expression in a process called Restructure, leading to the adoption in 1968 of a formal *Design for the Christian Church (Disciples of Christ)*. The *Design* structures us as one church with local congregational, regional, and general (including international) manifestations. These are not levels of power, as in a hierarchy of dominance and subordination. They are distinct but inseparable and interpenetrating spheres of association and activity, each relating to each other, serving with each other, and fulfilling certain special obligations on behalf of all. The services of every member of this one body, the church, are joined—so the Design states—by unbreakable covenantal ties of equality, complementarity, and mutual responsibility.

The initial fears of some that Restructure would spell the loss of important freedoms to a new, larger form of organization proved over time to be unfounded. Yet Restructure did bring changes, and it has served Disciples well in many respects. Our covenantal polity has enabled us to embrace many and varied ministries as our own. Our church has become more representative in its organization. For example, prior to Restructure, any and all could attend state and international meetings and then vote. Now most of these meetings, and our General Assembly particularly, provide for voting representatives from congregations and regions. Any who register may speak, but only voting representatives can vote. The weight of responsibility for oversight of our churchwide ministry shifted from individual discretion alone to collective decision-making and accountability. Above all, under the Design we proclaim that we are united as one church whose varied members, viewpoints, and services contribute to the life of the whole, not just an assortment of individuals, congregations, and organizations in occasional affiliation.

This is not to say that our church's health is problem-free. Not even a covenantal polity provides immunity from fallibility and fallenness. Our diversity of opinion—a historic hallmark of Disciples and a resource of great potential—leads at times to timidity and confusion and at times to factionalism and acrimony. The inclination to vie for power and prestige persists, and struggles for turf control are played out among and within our structures. Some in our church experience marginalization, powerlessness, even oppression. Certainly women and people of color still encounter barriers to full participation and equal opportunity. Our church has not yet vanquished prejudice or eliminated power elites. Challenges of ministering with covenantal faithfulness to God's Gospel in Jesus Christ for the sake of the world face us at every turn.

This quick review of history reminds us that the question of the church's true identity has been a serious concern of Disciples in the past, and several times subjected to probing churchwide examination. It also reminds us how much time has passed since our church last dealt with the question in a deliberate way.

The Contemporary Context

Since the days of Restructure, people have walked on the moon, torn down the Berlin wall and redrawn the map of Europe, ended apartheid, entered into a "global economy," and ushered in a communications revolution. The population center of world Christianity itself has shifted from Europe and North America to other continents. Many new theological emphases including theologies of liberation, have emerged within the churches. An awareness of the diversity of cultures and religions is a striking reality in our times.

Our thinking about the church must take note of changing circumstances in which we find ourselves. Of the many to be considered, we cite a few.

The context of diversity and globalization. Several trends are simply matters of fact to be kept in mind, such as the increasing racial-ethnic, cultural, and religious diversity of the United States population and the "globalization" of experience due to such things as international information networks and faster transportation. The key point to be made, however, is more fundamental. We are already in a period marked by the coexistence within North American society itself of deep and honest differences, even among those most dedicated to the church, about interpreting life's reality. This diversity can be a source of the church's renewal, reminding us that the church is to be a community embracing "Jew and Greek, male and female, slave and free." Certainly insights arising from groups of people who have been excluded from leadership in the church and society in the past are needed to enrich our understanding of the church. Still, the new context puts difficult questions before us each and all. How are we to discern the truth and give a persuasive account of it in the midst of so many differing voices and perspectives? How can we hold together as communities when common purpose seems so hard to find?

A new hunger for spiritual depth and community. Evidence abounds of widespread disenchantment with the individualism, shallowness, moral confusion, and secularism of our times. Many set out in quest of "roots," "connections," and "something more in life." The quest has led some to a new, or renewed, commitment as Christians. Others have been led elsewhere, or wander without apparent direction. The questing itself, however, calls to mind what is spoken of in the Christian heritage as that restlessness of the heart which finds its true peace only in God. The church should not tailor its message or life to consumer tastes. Yet it must take seriously and seek to address the longings for spiritual depth and community among people, many of whom have limited knowledge of the Christian story.

Threats to the future of the planet. Since 1988, the "Doomsday Clock" of nuclear destruction has been turned back, but many threats remain. The world is marked by massive poverty and periodic famine; by pollution, deforestation, and other indications of environmental degradation; by pain, injustice, and oppression inflicted upon masses of people, especially racial-ethnic minorities and women on every continent; and by savage conflict involving terrorism and ever-more sophisticated weaponry following the post–Cold War breakup of nation states. If the church is called to be a sign of God's justice and peace, then our understanding of the church dare not ignore or minimize these developments.

A "crisis" of mainline Christianity. The phrase is headline news; its meaning, well-known and well-documented: a decline in numbers and money, and apparent failure of nerve; a loss of cultural influence; the erosion of established channels for the flow of mission funds; a reliance on local (chiefly congregational) associations as the preferred carriers of identity and mission; a growing percentage of unchurched among those born into so-called "mainline churches"; and a disturbing factiousness within the churches themselves. Disciples have firsthand experience of this social trend: it has already led us to make some response and to anticipate more to come. In fact, the greatest danger here may be that in panic reaction to the immediacy of the crisis we will jettison some things and grasp onto others without adequately evaluating the impact of our actions in light of our best understanding of the church's true identity.

The Church, A Question of Faith Seeking Understanding

Analysis of its heritage and current situation teach us a great deal about our church— about who, what, and where we are. But it will not suffice to look at our church alone and make historical and sociological observations about its condition in the world. Indeed, if this is all we were to do, we would never come to an adequate understanding of the meaning of church. Why is this?

Faith leads Disciples to learn more about the purpose of his church than we can ever possibly know by looking at ourselves alone.

One reason is that the Christian Church (Disciples of Christ) is only one of "ordered communities of disciples" (*Design*, ¶ 2) in which the Universal Church of Jesus Christ appears. Its past and present are only one small part of the life of the church as a whole. Faith in Jesus Christ leads

Disciples to seek to learn *more* about the nature and purpose of *his* church than we can possibly ever know by looking at ourselves alone.

The other reason is that the question of the identity of the church is a question of *faith*. As such, it can never be answered rightly by examining churches from the viewpoint of history, sociology, politics, economics, or culture alone. Legislatures, law courts, tax codes, news media, telephone directories, political strategists, market analysts, research scholars, and many others give certain groups the name "church" and assign them a place among other social institutions. In this sense we must recognize that the word "church" is not something that we and other Christians can control. Economic, political, and other social and cultural forces have always demonstrated their powers to define not only "church" but much of the rest of human life. Hence social scientific and similar investigations may grant us genuine and important insights about the church's placement in human cultures. But only when we are led by faith to seek the church's God-given identity can we gain a proper understanding of what the church is *truly* called to be. Faith seeks an understanding that requires a *normative* definition of the church: an account of what the Christian church is if and when it becomes what God calls it to be. Such an account is based on criteria (norms) set by the Gospel of Jesus Christ, not by "the world."

This is not to deny that the church is very much "in the world." On the contrary, if and when the church exists truly, it exists as some specific, historic community or communities of people in the world. It is important, then, that we try to be clear about the relationship between the church and the world. The word "world" has three distinct but interrelated meanings in the language of faith: (1) the world as the cosmos created by God; (2) the world as the sphere of human existence, activity, and relations—that is, human culture; (3) the world as the sphere of human existence, activity, and relations that is burdened, infected, and distorted by human sin. The church is a community (or community of communities) of people located *in* the world in all three senses of the term "world." The church is in God's cosmos, within specific human culture, and amid cultural conditions and forces that are burdened, infected, and distorted by sin. Further, the world enters into—shaping and otherwise influencing—the life of the church in innumerable ways. Thus we must say not only that the church is *in* the world but that the world is *in* the church.

The ever-present threats to the church's integrity are (1) that it will allow itself to be *defined* by the world in which it exists—embracing as its very own the identity the world gives to it, accepting the place and role assigned to it by the world, honoring and serving and conforming to the world and (2) that it will presume to define itself as a community apart from the world which is God's and into which God has called it. The ever-present challenge for the church is to be *in but not of the world*. The fact that the church is in the world and the world is in the church (in all three senses of "world") makes it an earthen vessel, and continually in need of reform, renewal, and God's grace. In order to identify what makes a church truly church, we cannot simply describe the worldly state of the church. We must instead give an account of our understanding of the church in light of faith in the Gospel, which is God's covenant of love in Jesus Christ—a reconciling love directed towards the world that God loves.

PART 2

Lessons from Scripture and Tradition

What has God called, and by the power of the Spirit empowered, the church of Jesus Christ to be, to say, and to do? To understand the church's God-given identity, we must seek to understand the church in light of faith in God's Good News in Jesus Christ. "Faith seeking understanding" is a task that the church calls "theology." Thus our search for the church's true identity is a distinctively theological undertaking rather than a report of current church affairs. In this undertaking, we will look first and foremost for guidance from the Scriptures, exploring several prominent biblical images with decisive significance for an adequate understanding of the church. We will then look at what are commonly called the four historic ecumenical "marks" of the church. Finally, with these materials in mind, we examine the distinctive social character of the church.

The Witness of Scripture

Why do we turn to the Scriptures? Disciples have certainly always done so, and by this means (as well as many others) we acknowledge our participation in the one, Universal Church of Jesus Christ. But the church's reliance upon Scripture is due to more than custom alone. The call that the church is to heed is a call from God—God's self-communicating

Word—in the history of Israel, in Jesus Christ, and in the birth of the church itself by the power of the Holy Spirit. The Holy Scriptures witness to this Word through the testimony of the faithful of ancient Israel and the ancient church. This Word, which calls persons to faith and the church into being, is to be heard and heeded still through the scriptural writings of their testimony—and hence the church affirms the Scriptures to be of unique and normative significance for its own life and witness.

We seek, then, to understand what Scripture teaches regarding the community that God calls to be church. Diverse as it is, Scripture is emphatic on certain points. The church is a community called forth by God—the faith of Israel at its roots, the Gospel of God's covenant of love in Christ Jesus its cornerstone, the Holy Spirit its animating power, and the fulfillment of Jesus' prayer "that they all may be one" (John 17:21) its hope and goal. Such statements attest to essentials of the church's identity. But Scripture does not set forth any one, detailed, and complete blueprint for living out this identity. It provides, instead, many snapshots of Christian origins and an array of images of communities of faith which, taken together, are touchstones for Christian reflection. One biblical scholar has identified more than ninety such images, including the bride of Christ, the branches of a vine, disciples, salt of the earth, new creation, household of God, and holy temple.

These scriptural images and themes—as well as the ecumenical marks derived from the biblical witness—form an indispensable framework for the life of the church through history and for our reflections. The identity of the church is shaped and corrected by these images and marks as each generation of Christians accepts the task of interpreting them as wisely and adequately as possible for its own time and place. The church today, for example, is compelled to ask anew what the church of Corinth considered in the first century: how is the community of faith which we know like or unlike a body of many parts that sometimes hurts and sometimes rejoices, which sometimes squabbles bitterly and sometimes responds to the Spirit in common rhythm?

Biblical images and the ecumenical marks alike convey a normative definition of the church.

It should be noted that the biblical images and the ecumenical marks alike highlight what God has *called* the church to be, and hence they convey a normative definition of the church by describing Christian communities in terms of what they *already are* and *are not yet*. Again, Paul's letters to the Corinthian Christians illustrate the point. Paul dared them to believe that God in Christ was so present among them that their common life was like "the body of Christ." Yet he also urged that they anticipate a future glory of life in God that was immeasurably fuller than anything they could begin to know now. This was demanding, even audacious, counsel. Paul taught them that they—a faltering, squabbling community—were a continuation of Christ's ministry and an embodiment of God's grace, among whom the Spirit dwelt.

When considering biblical images and ecumenical marks of the church, readers today may be tempted to exclaim, "But that's not the way the church really lives." They would not be altogether wrong. The church has often been triumphalistic, believing that it and its duly appointed officers alone control sure and true access to the divine, when it should have been humble. It has often been timid, neglecting those who cry out in hunger and thirst (Matthew 25), when it should have been bold in seeking Christ in the outcast. At its best, however, the church welcomes these images and marks as a way of measuring and correcting the course of its common life. To put the matter even more directly, unless we respond soberly and humbly to Scripture's demanding witness that the Holy God dwells within and over our often faltering communities and institutions, we will not gain a true understanding of the church in our time and place.

Three key images—around which many others are clustered—command attention here, both because of their prominence in Scripture and their importance throughout the church's history. We will consider images of the church as the people of God, the body of Christ, and the community of the Holy Spirit. In each case, a passage of Scripture will sound the theme before it is opened up for discussion.

The People of God. "You are a chosen race, a royal priesthood, a holy nation, God's own people… Once you were not a people, but now you are God's people; once you had not received mercy, but now you have received mercy" (1 Peter 2:9–10).

To recognize that we are the people of God is to acknowledge, first of all, that the church is a gift and creation of God, not a community of our own making. Members of the church are incorporated into the people of God not because of who we are or what we have done but because of what God has made of us and done for us in Jesus Christ. This is why we, as sinners who by God's grace have become Christians, are humbly thankful to God and, out of genuine caring and overflowing joy rather than pride, proclaim God's Good News in Jesus Christ to other sinners. This is also why individuals and groups who are unlike, and even opposed to one another, in other respects find themselves brought together by the Gospel in the church. We are a people graciously constituted by God, not an institution built on entrance requirements of our own making.

This image reminds us, second, of our continuity with Israel, the community whom God has claimed "to be his people, his treasured possession" (Deuteronomy 7:6). When Christians assume that the church has now taken over the calling once given to Israel, we miss the point that 1 Peter is making. "Once you were not a people, but now you are God's people; once you had not received mercy, but now you have received mercy." To be called to be Christian, and hence called forth as the people of God, is to share in the mercy that God promises first to Israel and then extends even to "the gentiles" such as ourselves. "Peoples" are usually defined by a particular national boundary, language, or ethnic identity. This is not true of the church as the people of God. God's call creates Christians as a peculiar kind of people, a community that cuts across all worldly divisions and embraces persons from all the peoples of the world.

That God calls people into such a community is a demonstration of God's mercy. The mercy of God, repeatedly attested in the Scriptures, is referred to in *The Design for the Christian Church (Disciples of Christ)* as "the covenant of love which binds us to God and one another" (*Design*, ¶1). And in issuing this covenantal calling, like that of Israel, God proposes to bring forth a community that will be "a light to the nations" (Isaiah 49:6) and "good news of great joy to all the people" (Luke 2:11).

The Body of Christ. "For just as the body is one and has many members, and all the members of the body, though many, are one body, so it is with Christ. For in the one spirit we are all baptized into one body—Jews or Greeks, slaves or free—and we were all made to drink of one spirit" (1 Corinthians 12:12–13).

This image is perhaps so familiar that its full significance is often lost. It speaks of a unity so intimate that the loss of any member is a cause of great pain. But it also speaks of a unity constituted by an amazing diversity of gifts and functions. If the body were all hands or feet, says Paul, it would not be a body at all. Beyond that, it speaks of a unity such that each part can fulfill its intended purpose only by working in harmonious cooperation with the others. Interdependence—diverse members working for "the common good" (1 Corinthians 12:7)—here means, also, that none of us can tell another in the church "I have no need of you." It speaks of a unity such that "if one member suffers, all suffer together with it; if one member is honored, all rejoice with it" (1 Corinthians 12:26).

The church, however, is here spoken of not merely as a body but as the body of Christ. His body, "given for us," defines the nature of our life together—a life that is a continuation of his ministry in the world. This ministry is, in addition to preaching and teaching, a ministry of compassion, intercession, and self-giving service on behalf of the true well-being of others. That *this* is what it means to be the body of Christ is attested in the sacramental meal we call the Lord's Supper: "The Bread which we break, is it not a participation in the body of Christ? Because there is one Lord, we who are many are one body, for we all partake of the same loaf." (1 Corinthians 10:16–17). And because the church is *his* body, Jesus Christ is ultimate authority for the community of faith.

The Community of the Holy Spirit. "You will receive power when the Holy Spirit has come upon you, and you will be my witnesses in Jerusalem, in all Judea and Samaria, and to the ends of the earth." "When the day of Pentecost had come they were all together in one place. And suddenly from Heaven there came a sound like the rush of a violent win… All of them were filled with the Holy Spirit, and began to speak in other languages, as the Spirit gave them ability." (Acts 1:8; 2:1–4)

The story of Pentecost shows a double movement that characterizes our life in the church: the disciples were brought together through the Spirit's presence and sent out for mission through the Spirit's power. The Spirit who moved across the waters of creation moves creatively through the church; its community-creating power multiplies understanding and contrasts vividly to the confusion of tongues and fragmentation of community in the story of Babel. We are again reminded that it is God who directs our life as a community of faith. When the church submits itself, through disciplined study and discernment, to the leading of the Spirit, it is empowered for worship, authentic witness, and inclusive mission. Our common dependence on the Holy Spirit is often expressed in our worship services through the apostolic benediction, "The grace of the Lord Jesus Christ, the love of God, and the communion of the Holy Spirit be with all of you" (2 Corinthians 13:14).

Led by the Spirit, the church is empowered for worship, authentic witness, and inclusive mission.

These three images make us aware that the purpose and mission of the church is not defense or gain or entertainment or even comfort and companionship. It is based on and dedicated to God's covenant of love in Jesus Christ. And it is not a community that merely remembers God's love in the past or hopes for God's love in the future, but one called to *embody* that love daily, here and now. The embodiment of a love such as this in and by the church is made possible by God's self-giving, reconciling life in Jesus Christ, which grants freedom from slavery to sin and power for a new, redemptive course of life. To be a Christian, a disciple of Christ, is to participate in the community of his disciples, exhibiting the reconciling, liberating, and redemptive power of God in the world. The community called to be church is *itself* part of God's Good News in Jesus Christ.

Further, these images indicate that the life of the church is bound up with the very life of God and, thus, reflects the nature of the God upon whom it depends. God is the one who forms us as a people, who calls and reconciles us in Jesus Christ, and who sustains and leads us through the Holy Spirit. In keeping with the scriptural images of the church as the people of *God*, the body of *Christ*, and the community of the *Holy Spirit*, Disciples confess with the church throughout the ages the reality of the living God: the One God—Father, Son, and Holy Spirit; the One God—Creator, Redeemer, and Sustainer of the world. We confess, with humility and boldness, that Christian life together as church begins and ends in the gracious fullness of God.

What is affirmed by these three images of the church, as elsewhere in Scripture and Tradition, is the threefold self-revelation of the One God as gracious love in the creation and the history of Israel, in Jesus Christ, and in the calling of the church through the power of the Holy Spirit. Among Disciples, this affirmation is made in solemn moments of worship, most notably by the threefold formula used at the time of baptism. Christians must recognize the inadequacy of our human efforts to find words capable of expressing the reality of the living God. Yet we must also recognize that the church is called to witness to this reality nonetheless—and this means seeking to witness to this reality in its fullness.

To do so here, we will speak of the threefold self-revelation or self-communication of the One God and on occasion, as an apt synonym, of "the living triune God." The point that is being affirmed may, of course, find expression by the use of other terms, as indeed it has in the witness of the Disciples and the worldwide church. The strengths as well as the limits of the language Christians use to speak of God always demand careful consideration. In any case, the ministry of our church can only be enriched when Disciples learn more about the language of affirmation in the heritage of the worldwide church and so gain a more vital sense of its meaning and usefulness.

Four Ecumenical Marks of the Church

Ever since the first Council of Constantinople in A.D. 381, Christians have confessed in what is called the Nicene Creed that the church is "one, holy, catholic, and apostolic." Comprised of four scriptural terms, this affirmation of "the marks of the church" has come into widespread, honored use among Protestant, Orthodox, and Roman Catholic Christians over the centuries. The phrase "the four marks of the church" appears in Disciples teaching materials only occasionally, but the four marks themselves are certainly familiar to Disciples, who have been—and are—passionately concerned for the church's unity, holiness, wholeness (or catholicity), and continuity with the message of the apostles.

Disciples are passionately concerned for the church's unity, holiness, wholeness, and continuity with the apostles.

The Church is One. The oneness of the church is first and finally a gift of God which creates unity amid diversity. As a unity amid diversity, the oneness of the church refers not to total uniformity but to utter inseparability. It is a oneness which is organic, recognizing, celebrating, and depending upon the diverse character of the many members who are brought into unity by God's grace in Jesus Christ. It is also a oneness which is visible, extending beyond warm feelings of affection to become plain for all to see in the church's acts of confessing its faith, celebrating the sacraments, caring for one another, and ministering to others in the world.

In ecumenical discussion today, the favored term for speaking of the church's oneness is *koinonia*—a Greek word usually translated as fellowship or participation or communion (and underlying the image of the church as the community of the Spirit). The term reminds us that our communion with one another is rooted in our shared communion with Christ Jesus. Because the church is one, Christians are called to contend against racism, sexism, economic oppression, militant nationalism, and other forces which divide the followers of Christ. Because the church is one, the burden of proof always rests with those who hold that the purity of their teaching or practice justifies their separation from other parts of the body.

In New Testament usage, *koinonia* focuses our attention on our relatedness, that is, on the way we are actually present with and concerned for one another. Indeed, it was the term Paul used to refer to the collection he was gathering from the churches for the support of "the poor" in Jerusalem. Thus, *koinonia* is a word having to do with communion in the dynamic sense of an ever-growing process of exhibiting love for one another even as Christ has loved us.

The Church is Holy. The holiness of the church stems solely from God's gracious presence in its midst, a presence that is not a cause for boasting but an occasion for humble thanks. Indeed, an acknowledgement that the church is holy should lead us to confess our sinfulness and to recognize that our life as a community is dependent on God's grace and forgiveness.

This community of forgiven sinners is also called to costly obedience in response to grace, to ministry in the world for the sake of the Holy One we worship (a point Disciples seek to highlight by the practice of believers' baptism). The church understands itself to be a community that nurtures and practices the virtues of faith, hope, and love. In a world in which these virtues are often scorned, these practices can—and at times do—set the church in opposition to the surrounding culture. Yet the holiness of the church is most truly expressed, Disciples have maintained, through continued engagement with the world for the sake of its transformation rather than withdrawal from it. In sum Christians are called to be a people ever-becoming holy and sanctified through their maturation in the Christian life.

The Church is Catholic. The term "catholic" comes from a Greek word meaning "whole." It has generally been used to signify the whole faith as opposed to that which is partial or one-sided and so too the whole church as opposed to that which is provincial or divisive. In one of its senses, then, it is closely associated with a word much more familiar to Disciples—ecumenical, which highlights the worldwide comprehensiveness of Christian faith. "Catholic" also means being inclusive of people of all sorts and conditions. All of these references are reminders that exclusivism always reflects an over-emphasis on either some part of the whole faith or some part of the whole church, and thus betrays the church's true identity.

This mark of the church points us toward a crucial tension: the church is at once local and universal. The community that gathers faithfully in each place to break bread and share life in memory of Jesus Christ is truly the church catholic—an expression here and now of the church's wholeness and integrity. They express this by joining the whole church in confessing the one faith, by sharing in one baptism, participating in the one ministry of Jesus Christ. The Lord's Table around which we gather extends beyond our local place of worship to encircle the world and to span the ages of time, because the faith we confess binds us in a universal fellowship. In other words, each congregation is truly church, but it cannot be this apart from its unity with the sisters and brothers in Christ gathered as worshipping and serving communities in other times and places.

The Church is Apostolic. The church is apostolic when it is faithful to the Gospel message transmitted to the church through the proclamation of the apostles. This mark is a way of acknowledging that we did not invent the Gospel, but received it. It attests that the church we know is "built on the foundation of the apostles and prophets, Jesus Christ being the chief cornerstone" (Ephesians 2:20). Concern for the apostolicity of the church reminds us of the continuity of the church from its beginnings to the present day, and it keeps us from adapting too easily to the spirit of our particular age.

Some parts of the church have historically placed great emphasis on the transmission of ministerial authority—"apostolic succession"—as the chief *sign* of apostolicity. Certainly ordination invests ministers with special responsibility to teach the apostolic faith. But Disciples emphasize, in line with their Protestant heritage as well as ecumenical discussion, that apostolicity is expressed by the whole church, not just its ordained ministry, as we turn again and again to interpret the apostolic witness of Scripture. To be apostolic is not assured by reproducing every detail of the church of the apostles; it requires that we commit to live out the Gospel (which we received from the apostles) in our times, even as those in apostolic times sought, through the power of God's spirit, to live it out in theirs.

There is another meaning to this mark of the church. An apostle is literally one who is "sent forth." The apostles were those commissioned for missionary witness in the name of Jesus Christ—caring for the poor, the suffering, those bereft of hope, the unbelievers. When Disciples emphasize that apostolicity is expressed by the whole church (joined together as one "priesthood of all believers"), not just its ordained ministry, we are committing ourselves as individuals and as a whole to go forth and make the Gospel known by our words and deeds to all the world.

These biblical images and ecumenical marks provide invaluable insights into the true identity of the church. Yet not even they tell all there is to be told. Other terms sometimes put the same points in fresh ways and sometimes offer added insight. One recent study suggests a number of images of the church which are especially instructive for our age, such as the church as a caring community, a community of and for the poor, and a community of repentance. The image of the "Believers' church" highlights the importance of responsible commitment to Christ on the part of each individual, lest church membership come to mean little more than a function of background, birth, or social status. Historic peace churches, e.g., Friends and Brethren, have long argued that peace-making is an essential mark of the community called forth by the Prince of Peace.

The Eschatological and Social Character of the Church

One additional scriptural theme deserves special attention, we believe, because it sets all the others in proper perspective: the church as an eschatological community. Eschatology is based on the Greek word *eschaton*, meaning "the end time" or "final things," when God's intended purposes for creation come to ultimate fulfillment. The church is rightly concerned to recall and celebrate what God has done in the past. It is rightly concerned for the nurture and well-being of its own members, and also rightly concerned to mend and heal the present brokenness of the world. Yet the Gospel of Jesus Christ always points the church beyond the past and beyond the present and indeed beyond itself—toward the reign of God.

To be an eschatological community is to live in anticipation of that day when God's promise of shalom for all creation is fulfilled. Such a community is at once a pledge of God's intention for the world and a provisional demonstration of God's power to make it happen. Few humans have even dreamed of a community in which Jew and Greek, slave and free, male and female live in truly committed relations of love, honoring one another's uniqueness, dignity, and equality. The church, despite its sinfulness, is called and empowered to be just such a community.

The church which understands itself as an eschatological community will not confuse itself with the reign of God. Indeed, precisely because the church is God's eschatological community, it will not make itself the center of its message and its activity but will point beyond itself to God's designs for history and creation. It will not give the impression that its teachings and structures are everlasting but will witness to the hope of God's everlasting reign. When the church is truly church, its life overflows with such eschatological hope.

The Social Character of the Christian Life. In discussing lessons from Scripture and Tradition, we have repeatedly affirmed that the church is a *community* of persons. The church is often spoken of in this way in church circles—so often that the import of the phrase is perhaps hardly noted. A few of its important implications deserve comment.

The church is the *community* of Christ's faithful, not the places or the buildings in which that community gathers. To "go to church" for worship, weddings, and other activities is to participate in the witness of this community of God. Unless this witness is made, activities are taking place in the church's *building* rather than *in the church*. A somewhat less sharp and more subtle but equally significant distinction is to be made between the community of faith and the propertied, legally incorporated "institutional entities" called churches. Neither Scripture nor the marks of the church define the church in such terms. Scripture gives us clues as to how the early church ordered its life, but it does not specify one particular form of organization necessary for all subsequent generations. From its multifaceted materials, we conclude that the church is a re-ordering of human life into a *community* and that this community bears the responsibility for developing institutional structures by which to carry out its witness to the Gospel in the world.

Issues relating to the church's development of institutional structures will be dealt with at a later point (Part 4). Here, however, we focus on the communal character of the church. What we can say on the basis of Scripture is that the Gospel has the power to reform human relationships into a shared social life with a distinctive character shaped by God's work of reconciliation, liberation, and redemption. The distinctive character of this social life can be summarized by stating that the church is:

- a community of love in which members join in common devotion to the upbuilding of the whole body;

- a community of unity amid diversity in which the particularity of each (in every respect excepting our sins) is received as a gift of grace to be shared;
- a community of both local and universal reach, linking our "Hometown Christian Church" to faithful followers of Christ in Kenya, Russia, and elsewhere and linking the twentieth-century church to that of the first century and to that of centuries yet to come;
- a community of shared ministry in the name of Jesus Christ in keeping with his work of reconciliation, liberation, and redemption.

These four features of the distinctive social character of the church are constitutive elements of church life. To the extent they are lacking, the church falls short of its distinctive social character of the church are constitutive elements of church life. To the extent they are lacking, the church falls short of its God-given calling. The fact that Christianity is inherently social, that the Gospel is news with community-creating power, has often proved difficult for Christians to appreciate. Our preference, were God to have asked our advice, may well have been for a message that comes only as a set of simple moral instructions or as one that comes directly into our hearts. Surely it complicates matters that in accepting Christ we have to accept other Christians as well. Our wish might well have been for a community untroubled by diversity, without mutual respect and care, or perhaps devoted to some work other than reconciliation, liberation, and redemption. In sum, the church depicted in Scripture presents us with obligations and challenges we might readily forgo. But God, we must confess finally and in truth, has not willed that this be so. The true identity of the church is not a proposal on which we get to vote. It is a given to which we are to respond with praise and faithfulness to God.

The identity of the church is a given to which we are to respond with praise and faithfulness to God.

Christians have also never found it easy to deal with the "mixed" reality of the church: a community that is *already* a sign of God's purposes but *not yet* fully conformed to God's will, a community called to be in the world but not altogether of it. We are constantly tempted to release the tension by focusing on one side or the other. Some Christians tend to divinize the church, making exaggerated claims about the power, glory, and perfection of its members or its visible institutions. Others tend to think too little of the church, describing it merely in terms of its programs, functions, or organization. The images and marks we have explored remind us that both tendencies are misunderstandings of the church's true identity.

The Gospel that Calls the Church to Life

Our discussion of the images, the marks, and the social character of the church could of course be extended. Its various points might be reordered, put differently, supplemented by other materials, and, if corrections are in order, improved upon. This is as it should be, for continued study and churchwide dialogue can surely aid all of us in our common efforts to understand the true identity of the church. Yet some points that have emerged here are, we believe, so fundamental and so amply warranted as to be beyond all reasonable doubt. Primary among them is this: in light of the witness of Scripture, faithful Christians realize that the church is a community of persons called into being by the Gospel of Jesus Christ.

If the church is to have any say in its own self-definition in the midst of the reigning cultural powers, it is necessary to recover the sense of the church as *called* into being by the Gospel of Jesus Christ. Whenever the church's awareness of this calling—and indeed of its distinctiveness—dims or wavers, the church loses its moorings, drifts off course, and falls prey to one or another of the identities conferred by and bound to its surrounding culture. We can become clear about church's true identity only when we become clear about the meaning of the Gospel of Jesus Christ.

Here, then, we must insist that the Gospel cannot be separated from Jesus Christ. Whenever the church hedges on this point or settles on some other "gospel," it reveals that it is confused in its understanding of its identity, and hence everything it undertakes to be and to say and to do becomes suspect. It seems painfully evident that North American churches at least are suffering just such an "identity crisis." Critical distinctions—those, e.g., between righteousness and self-righteousness, between popularity and faithfulness, and between "No Creed but Christ" and "No Creed or Any Creed, as you please"—are frequently overlooked.

What, then, is the Gospel of Jesus Christ? Of course, the whole of the church's theology is but an attempt to answer and then explain its answer to the question. Christians surely realize that the Gospel is more than a matter of words and ideas. It is the power as well as the message from God, and so cannot be reduced to or captured in any formula. Yet the church dare not, has not, and finally cannot avoid acknowledging the Gospel. Disciples do so by confessing, "Jesus is the Christ, the Son of the Living God, and Lord and Savior of the world." In making this confession, the church dare not and finally cannot avoid the task of offering our best understanding of what these words mean, i.e., the content of the Gospel.

Let us propose, then, the following as a succinct summary of the Gospel:

> The Gospel of Jesus Christ is the Good News that the God of Israel, the creator of all things, has in freedom and love identified God's being and life with the life, death, and resurrection of Jesus of Nazareth, God's Son, to enact and reveal God's gracious reconciliation of sinful humanity to Godself, and calls humanity through the Holy Spirit to participate in God's liberative and redemptive work by acknowledging God's reconciliation, repenting of its sin, receiving the gift of freedom, realizing authentic community by loving the neighbor and the enemy, caring for the whole creation, and living in hopeful anticipation of

the final triumph of the gracious God as the Ultimate Companion of all creatures.

What is affirmed in this statement has already been touched on at least briefly in the course of discussion so far. It will guide all that we have to say about the church from this point on.

PART 3

The Defining Signs of the Church's Identity

In this part, we focus on the relationship between the Gospel's call to life and mission and the various practices which the church undertakes in fulfilling this calling. Our goal is to understand what a community of people actually is and says and does when it is *truly* the church of Jesus Christ. Are there defining signs we should look for? The lessons we have gained from Scripture and Tradition—chief among them, our summary statement of the Gospel itself—will inform and direct our efforts to answer this question. We will look, then, for defining signs of the church's true identity in the way a community acknowledges, lives out, and communicates its God-given life and mission.

The Gospel's Call to Life and Mission

The testimony of Scripture makes clear that Christian community is called into being by the Good News of God in Jesus Christ through the Holy Spirit. The church exists because it has been called out and gathered together by the gracious, reconciling, self-revealing presence of God in Jesus Christ through the movement of the Holy Spirit. This call gives to the church not only its life but also its reason for living: its distinctive purpose, its defining mission, is to witness in word and deed to the living triune God.

The Gospel which calls the church to life and mission defines its identity as well. Acknowledging that it is brought forth into life and sent forth for mission by its calling from God is constitutive of the church's identity. The church embodies this acknowledgment in words and deeds; indeed the church can be said to live in and through its practices of faithful witness to God's call. Therefore, the defining signs of the church's identity are to be sought and found among those activities in which a community acknowledges its calling from God by witnessing to God on the basis of the Gospel of Jesus Christ.

What do we mean by witness? First, it is a *living testimony* to the living triune God. A vital awareness of being called and sent out, by the power of the Spirit, on a mission of witnessing to the wondrous, gracious mystery of God's redemptive actions in the history of Israel and in Jesus of Nazareth suffuses the New Testament. The community called to be church actively engages in this mission of witness to the reality of the one God. The church has its true life only in the complex richness of its ongoing response to God's call to life and mission. Where acts of living witness are missing, there is actually no true church.

Second, the church witnesses to God by *word and deed*. Both words and deeds are proper and necessary. Indeed, they are inseparable, for word without deed is hypocritical, vain, deadly, and a lie, and deed without word loses its defining content, intention, and luminosity. The two are also intertwined insofar as the church's deeds of witness speak loudly and its words of witness are themselves activities, deeds.

Third, the church engages in its mission of witness *for the sake, the benefit, of the world*. It is this world—past, present, and future—which God loves with an unfathomably gracious, reconciling love that liberates and redeems. The church is a community of persons who, in saying "yes" to the Gospel of Jesus Christ, know that by God's mercy their own lives are liberated and are being redeemed. But they know too that the church does not exist simply for itself or as an end in itself, for God's loving mercy is not for themselves alone but for the whole world. Thus the church bears witness to God's love *for* the world.

That said, we can proceed to identify the defining signs of the church among its acts of witness in word and deed. We will call these acts *practices of the church in the world*. This way of expressing the matter highlights that these are human activities, that they are regularly performed, and that they always take place in some specific historical setting, communal tradition, and social location. These practices are the means by which the church exhibits the signs of its identity; that is, by engaging in them the church becomes and makes itself known as being truly church. They are also the abiding *means of grace* by which the Holy Spirit sustains the life of the church as the pilgrim people who witness to the gracious life of God.

We will describe the signs in only broad strokes. Let us begin by distinguishing between two sorts of activities by which the church carries out its mission of witness to the Gospel: *nurturing practices* and the *outreach practices*. Nurturing practices are activities of the church which are directed primarily toward the community itself, toward the cultivation, the upbuilding, of its faith. Outreach practices are activities of the church which are directed primarily outward, toward the transformation of the world.

The church lives in the dynamic interaction between nurturing itself for witness and engaging the world.

This distinction is not meant to imply sharp boundaries between these practices. On the contrary, we must insist that the church lives in the dynamic interaction between nurturing itself for witness and engaging the world in concrete works of love for the benefit of the world. Most church practices have dual faces, one directed toward the community of faith and the other directed toward the world. In any case, in witnessing to and for the world, the church is itself nurtured by the Spirit, and in the nurturing of its communal life, the church is witnessing to and for the world.

There is in addition a third group of church practices, necessary accompaniments of the church's nurturing and outreach practices. These are *administrative practices:* activities by which the church organizes itself for the fulfillment of its mission of witnessing through nurture and outreach.

Nurturing Practices: Worship, Education, and Communal Care

Looking first at the *nurturing practices* of the church, we can see three spheres of inner-church activity: *worship, education*, and *communal care*. We will discuss each in its turn, although we must stress that these are actually overlapping moments of the church's life which cannot be segmented and separated sharply. Moreover, they are always related to—shaped by and contributing to—the outreach activities that the church undertakes in and for the world.

Worship. The defining signs of the church found in worship are striking illustrations of how word and deed are intertwined in the life of the church. The community called into being by the Gospel of Jesus Christ is a community with a distinctive self-understanding. The call it hears is that of God's self-communicating Word in the history of Israel and in Jesus Christ as recorded in and transmitted to us through the writings of the Holy Scriptures. Through these writings the church receives not only the essential content of its faith but as it were the distinctive language of that faith—images, concepts, beliefs, teachings, and practices—which both shapes and critiques its own life. Therefore, two of the *defining signs* of the church are the *practices of listening to Scripture as the Word of God* and *of being called, authorized, shaped, and judged by this listening.*

The worship of the church is centered upon and formed around the Scriptural witness. Worship itself is fundamentally the activity of praising God as the Creator, Reconciler, and Redeemer of humanity and all of creation. In communal worship the church makes four other defining signs of its true identity: *it proclaims the Word heard in Scripture, it confesses its sin and embraces the forgiving grace of God, it celebrates God's gracious life in sacramental acts of*

Baptism and Holy Communion, and it communicates in prayer with God. The church worships by engaging in these multi-dimensional practices of praising and conforming to the living triune God.

Classic Protestant formulas spoke of the word and the sacraments as the only defining signs of the church, affirming, e.g., that the church is where the word is preached and heard and the sacraments administered according to the institution of Jesus Christ. To reformers like Luther and Calvin, this formula meant that hearing the word and receiving the sacraments in faith were events in which one participated in the person and work of Christ crucified. The effect of this participation was a radical re-orientation of one's life. One was drawn out—and wanted to be drawn out—of self, directed into right relationship with God and the neighbor, and so empowered to live in the world on behalf of others and the world.

In this sense, hearing the Word and participating in the sacraments embraces within itself the whole of the Christian life both personally and corporately. We acknowledge this connection between these practices and the whole of Christian life, and therefore affirm that word and sacrament are defining signs of the church. But recognizing that this connection is not everywhere acknowledged, we will specify other defining signs amid the church's nurturing, outreach, and administrative practices.

The proclamation of God's Word given in Israel, in Jesus Christ, and in the early church, as attested in Holy Scripture, is critical to the church's life. Where it is heard in faith people find that we are not our own but God's, we die to ourselves, and we are turned outward to the neighbor and the world. This is the central aim of the *sermon* in worship. But proclaiming the Word takes place in numerous other ways as well—whenever and wherever the testimony of the Scriptures shapes the life of the church.

Understanding "sacrament" to mean a living and effective "sign," we regard the celebration of the sacraments of baptism and the Lord's Supper as practices by which the life of the church is conformed to the gracious life of

God and the faithful are both called and drawn out of their bondage to themselves. In these practices, the church recalls and encounters here and now the wondrous grace of God in Jesus Christ.

Baptism is a sign of God's grace in Jesus Christ, an acknowledgement of that grace, and a promise to live in faithful—thankful and obedient—response to that grace. The church acts as community in baptism to recognize a person's entry into the life of faith as a life of witness to the grace of God lived in the church for the world. By our baptism we do not purchase the forgiveness of sin. Rather, we make a public acknowledgment of our dependence upon God's grace and our reliance on forgiveness and justification in Christ; we give thanks for the liberation of ourselves by faith in Christ; and we proclaim our commitment to live in thanksgiving for God's gift and on behalf of our neighbor and the world. In sum, in baptizing the new believer the church declares the grace of God, confirms the believer's commitment to Christ, and pledges to nurture the person in a life of faith.

In the celebration of *the Lord's Supper*, the church remembers God's act of reconciliation in the life, death, and resurrection of Jesus of Nazareth, and through the Spirit it receives the living grace of the crucified Christ. In this sacrament that makes present for the church the gift of God's transforming grace offered to all human beings, the church finds the center of its worship. The sacrament neither repeats the self-giving of Christ nor adds to it. It celebrates what Jesus Christ has already done, his continuing life in the Spirit for the church, and the coming of the reign of God. In the common realities of the bread and the fruit of the vine, the church knows itself sustained by the body and blood of Jesus Christ.

It is Christ Jesus, rather than the church or its officers, who invites the church to the Table, and the whole church is invited. In this act, the church is itself enacting the practice of being invited, of receiving through the Spirit God's gracious reconciliation of the world. And in being invited, the church is empowered to invite the whole world to know and receive God's reconciling love. In *being invited and in inviting,* the church also engages in the practice of *hoping in the Spirit* for that future with God in which the world will finally be redeemed. Hence, thanksgiving and hope are the persistent themes of this event.

Praying ceaselessly is another of the characteristic activities of worship. Praying is the individual and communal practice of intentional communication with God's graciously self-communicating life. The church prays in the name of Jesus Christ, and its practice of prayer expresses the conviction that God is living and loving—that God solicits, hears, is affected by, and responds to human prayer. In the many moments of praying, the church gives thanks and praise to God, confesses its sin, lifts petitions and supplications to God, seeks God's guidance, makes intercession for the world, listens silently in reverent openness, cries out in pained lamentation, and groans in "sighs too deep for words" (Rom. 8:26). In its practices of prayer the church makes another of the defining signs of its true identity in the world.

Without the regular celebration of the Lord's Supper, the church forgets its very life.

In the practices of worship the church finds its life nurtured by the living triune God. Without the practice of reading Scripture and proclaiming the Word heard therein, the church inevitably gives itself over to some other supposedly life-conferring and life-directing "good news." Without the confession of sin and reliance on the mercy of God's forgiveness, the church is tempted to become presumptuous and self-righteous. Without the celebration of baptism, the church forgets that the Gospel is a gift of God which brings about renewal of life and conversion from ways of sinning to a new way of living, a new self-understanding, and hope of life eternal. Without the regular celebration of the Lord's Supper, the church forgets that its very life depends upon the reconciling life, death, and resurrection of Jesus of Nazareth, the incarnate Son of God. Without prayer the church presumes to give itself its own guidance day by day and neglects to live intentionally before the loving Spirit who calls and directs the church into God's future. In these many acts of worship the church becomes truly church—but never in isolation from the outreach practices in which the church exists for the world.

Educative Practices. The practices of *educating and being educated* pervade the life of the faithful church. As a community of persons called into being by the Gospel and sent on a mission of witness, all the members of the community are called to be conformed in the totality of their lives to the living triune God. This is a conformity of faith. By its very nature faith seeks constantly and in every way possible to understand God more adequately, and so also to understand itself and the world rightly. Faith seeks understanding. This is true for each individual Christian and the community as a whole. Hence, faithfulness leads the church to engage in numerous practices by which it *teaches* both the what and the how of faith: what the church most fundamentally believes and understands about God, human life and destiny, and the world; and how persons live in the world sanctified lives of understanding and action in keeping with the ethics of grace. In a vital faith, the what and the how cannot be separated. The how is aimless without the what, and the what is abstract and detached without the how. No member of the church ever advances beyond the imperative of grace to learn—more fully and personally—how to live before God. Hence none of us can ever do without participating in the educative practices of the church. And the church can never assume that the task of educating its members in faith is altogether completed.

Although much Christian educating occurs indirectly through loving relationships, it is essential that the church engage in explicit practices of teaching the faith. From the enlightening and upbuilding power of preaching which explicates Scripture, to the intentionally designed classes and conversations dealing with faith's meaning, to the silent but wise observations of saintly examples in its midst, the church educates and is educated by the Spirit. The church's teaching of the faith is necessarily theological in character. And distinctively Christian education is impossible unless the church is a community of theological discourse—discourse in which all things are referred to, examined, and evaluated in the light of faith in the self-communicating life of God. When the church's discourse becomes empty or vain or unfocused or weakened by counterfeit substitutes, the church loses its capacity to educate persons in the faith which lives from the Gospel of Jesus Christ. The teaching of the faith is itself a witness to God, and as such one of the defining signs of the church's identity.

Additional defining signs of the church appear in those educative practices (carried on usually by speaking together) concerned with *being critically responsible for the authenticity and effectiveness of church witness*. This responsibility arises from the awareness that because the church is called by the Gospel, it is accountable to God and even questioned in its witnessing by the life of God. The church knows itself to be subject to constant questioning by God regarding whether its many practices of witness in word and deed are genuinely faithful to the Gospel of Jesus Christ and luminous, truthful, and transformative for the world. This questioning and answering goes on until the end of time. In the life of the church, responsible, theological questioning is a sign that the church is called, sent, disturbed, and enlivened by the Spirit of the living God.

Its educative task also makes it beneficial for the church to develop practices by which it can arrive from time to time at a common, public confession of its faith. Without these practices, the church is in danger of being tossed to and fro by the winds of public opinion: it exposes itself to outside forces because the vital center of its faith remains unacknowledged before the world and to itself. Such confessions are limited in scope, timely rather than timeless, and always reformable. They need not be considered as tests of fellowship or preconditions for church unity. Their chief value is instructional. They give focus to the church's efforts to educate its members with regard to the meaning of its calling in the midst of a clamorous and powerful world.

Communal Care. Worship and education are inseparable from the totality of ways in which the church is itself a community of mutual love engaging in practices of *communal caring*. As Christians, we love because we were first loved by God in Jesus Christ. Christian love is that peculiar openness and self-giving to another, which seeks the good of the other as one's neighbor before God. This love, and the practices of care that go with it, is always particularized—a loving of this person, these persons. In *loving one another through mutual self-giving and care,* the church attests that it is truly a *koinonia,* a fellowship and communion of mutual upbuilding. Without works of love within the community, the church is hardly capable of performing the works of love in and for the world to which it is surely called.

The love which Christians have for one another is what empowers love for the world of neighbors.

Indeed, the love which Christians have for one another, empowered as it is by the self-giving Spirit of God, is what empowers love for the world of neighbors and strangers. This communal love is neither exclusive nor restricted. In being open to the neighbor-in-the-church, the church becomes the school in which Christians are trained in loving the neighbor-in-the-world. In all these ways this communal love is an ethics of grace made possible by God's self-giving life in Jesus Christ. By ethics of grace we mean the imperatives of Christian living which spring from the forgiveness of sin and the justification by grace in Jesus Christ and which confer a liberating freedom for the neighbor and for God.

Outreach Practices: Evangelism, Vocation, Prophecy, and Projects of Love, Justice, and Peace

We turn now to the *outreach practices* of the church. At the outset we must recall that the church is a liberative community. The word "liberative" has two distinct but interrelated meanings. First, the church is a liberative community because the Gospel of Jesus Christ that calls it into being is liberating. Being liberated in Christ is rooted in the acknowledgement of God's forgiveness and justification of sinners in the life, death, and resurrection of Jesus Christ. In Jesus Christ, God's judgment is accomplished, and it is revealed that sin will not have the last word in determining the meaning and destiny of humanity. Christians—the church—are persons who say "yes" to this liberation in Christ and who experience by the Spirit newness of life and direction: they are granted release from the controlling force and ultimate consequences of sin.

Second, the church is a liberative community in that it is the bearer of a liberating witness in word and deed for the world. Even as the church celebrates the gracious liberation of God, it is called and sent to take this liberating good news to the world. Hence the faithful church is continually engaged in the liberative practices of witnessing to God's liberative and redemptive work. In all its life the church is engaged in the ethics of grace: an ethics which lives from God's grace and justification, which does not seek just reward, and which reaches out into the world by liberative works of love on behalf of the neighbor. These outreach works of love in and for the world are carried out in several different spheres of activity.

Evangelism. The first sphere to be mentioned is that of evangelism. The term "evangelism" refers to all of the church's efforts to take the Gospel to the world and invite the world to respond to this news with a renewal of life and a change of direction. Even though some practices of the churches have sullied and obscured the true meaning of evangelism, faithfulness to its calling requires that the church engage—responsibly—in the multiple *practices of sharing, interpreting, and applying the message of the Gospel of Jesus Christ for the world*. Making declarations about the Gospel is one form of evangelism. But evangelism also involves practices of *persuasively interpreting the Gospel in conversation with the world*. The church enters into dialogue with the world in the conviction that God loves the world and calls it into a redemptive relationship with God's own life. In undertaking this task, the church must speak in terms that the world can understand even as it preserves the distinctiveness of its own message.

Since evangelism aims at sharing the Gospel with others, care must be taken that the church is indeed sharing the Gospel and not something else. The church must continually test its evangelistic practices for possible contamination by the messages, interests, and values of any given controlling nation, class, racial-ethnic heritage, or gender. Further, the church must remember that although its evangelistic practices often involve speaking or writing, evangelism can never be separated from appropriate nonverbal works of love on behalf of the world.

In sum, though the church may be ashamed of certain forms of evangelism, past and present, it can never be ashamed of the Gospel itself, and the Gospel beckons the church to share the news of God's saving grace in Jesus Christ with the world which God loves. The church confesses, professes, and demonstrates in works of love the Good News of Jesus Christ to the world, and is not ashamed.

Daily Outreach. The second sphere of outreach practice is formed by the ways in which the individual Christian lives in the world day-by-day and witnesses to the reality of God for the particular neighbors and the particular social institutions we deal with. The Gospel calls each and every Christian to live in the world on behalf of our particular neighbors, seeking their good and standing caringly at their side. Although the worldly powers of privilege, enmity, fear, and violence tempt and threaten us, Christians find in the Gospel a freedom and courage to live for their neighbors in the world. Christians know that each person they meet and relate to each day is created and loved by God. *Practices of Christian caring for others* in their particularity and in specific circumstances are among the defining signs of the church's true identity in the world.

Prophecy. Outreach practices include prophetic practices of the church. In these practices the *church calls the principalities* *and powers of the world to account*, especially where the world is infected and distorted by sin, and names the oppressive and unjust arrangements of those powers. These prophetic practices have to be rooted in the Gospel of Jesus Christ, for sheer denunciation independent of the Gospel is neither truly Christian prophecy nor a pathway to genuine human reconciliation, liberation, and redemption. As prophet, the church speaks best for the oppressed when it seeks freedom, justice, and mercy for both the oppressed and the oppressor. Oppression is incompatible with the Gospel of peace, justice, and love. And being an oppressor is itself a form of slavery, for oppressors are captive to the illusion that the power of determining life, death, and destiny rests in their hands, not God's. Thus oppression is not good for anyone involved. Hence the church prophesies to the world by word and deed, and must continually engage in critical self-examination to detect and avoid various ways in which it collaborates with and supports the powers of injustice and oppression.

Projects of Love, Justice, and Peace. The fourth sphere of outreach practices is comprised of those communal and collaborative activities the church pursues in and for the world on behalf of the love, justice, and peace envisaged in Jesus' announcement of the kingdom of God. The reign of God itself will finally be realized through God's redemptive action alone. But the Gospel of the coming of this kingdom, which measures and judges all human kingdoms, calls for the church *to seek justice and peace and so to collaborate with others in specific projects in pursuit of these goals*. Yearning for the realization of God's peaceable kingdom of mutual love, the church moves with resilient hope toward the world through these work-projects. In its various locations, the church pursues projects which feed the hungry and empower the poor for full social participation in life's goods, which bring to the center of life those who are pushed to the margins by the principalities and powers of the world, and which enable persons to be nonviolent neighbor-keepers. Although these practices do not usher in the reign of God, they are signals of its coming, and they are further defining signs of the church's true identity. Communities which do not engage in such practices fall short in their witness to the Gospel of Jesus Christ.

All that we have said makes it clear that the tendency to pit the practices of nurture and outreach against one another—e.g., evangelism versus social involvement—is improper and harmful to the life of the church. These practices can no more be separated from one another than witness in word and witness in deed. And in its outreach practices especially the church confesses, professes, and demonstrates its hope for the world's redemption, and its witness to hope pulls the church forward into God's future for the world. By the multiplicity of its nurturing and outreach practices the church itself becomes a signal, a parable, of the coming reign of God.

Administrative Practices

We turn now to the *administrative practices* by which the church organizes itself for its distinctive mission of witness in nurture and outreach. Historically the churches have disagreed about the organization and proper administration of church life. We will address many key concerns relating to this topic—in the Christian Church (Disciples of Christ) in particular—in the next section of this report, Part 4: Issues of Relationship and Structure. Hence the aim here will be limited: we wish to clarify in which respect(s) administrative practices are among the defining signs of the church.

The administering of church is an unavoidable necessity, and its proper role is to equip the whole church to fulfill its calling as the people *(laos)* of God. And the whole church is organizationally involved in the ministry of witness to God for the benefit of the world. Every church member has a vocation of witness. Yet the church's practices of nurture and outreach can only be sustained through a social organization which prepares, arranges for, teaches, facilitates, and coordinates these practices. Hence, *administering* this social network of persons and practices and the relationships between the two is integral to the church's capacity for faithful witness. For this reason the church entrusts tasks of administrative leadership to certain of its members, the goal of which is to enable the whole church to fulfill its God-given calling.

In light of historic, and current, disputes about administrative leadership in the church, we must stress two points that follow from this account. First, since the church's administrative organization is to enable the whole church to fulfill its calling, it is also secondary to and judged by that calling. Second, since the church's administrative organization is secondary and judged by the church's calling, the church is not defined as church by any particular arrangement of offices, officers, or process of leadership selection.

For the sake of this whole ministry, and in conformity to the servanthood of Jesus Christ, the Spirit of God from time to time calls out particular persons suitable for functions and tasks of servant leadership. Some of these servant leaders are formally ordained by the church as persons who represent to the church its own identity and mission in Jesus Christ and in this capacity assume certain specific ongoing responsibilities of leadership. It is in the practices of *ordaining-by the-church* and the practices of persons *providing servant-leadership* that the church exhibits further defining signs of its God-given identity. But the signs are in these practices, not in the characteristics of the persons or their offices.

These ordained leaders go by various names in Scripture and Tradition, e.g., pastor, elder, bishop, priest, deacon, or simply minister. Whatever their title, they are called by the Spirit and examined, approved, and ordained by the church to serve as representative ministers entrusted with servant-leadership roles in many of the practices of the church's witness. The church seeks out for its ordained ministries those most fitting to fulfill them, and fitness to serve cannot be determined on the basis of racial-ethnic heritage, class, or gender.

Trained in sound biblical interpretation, critically aware of the traditions and practices of the church, adept and discerning in their articulation of the Gospel, and skilled in practices of communal leadership and care, ordained ministers are invested by the church with real authority and responsibilities. Leading the community in worship through preaching and sacramental celebration, the minister regularly engages in practices of worship administration. As wise and educated theologian for the church, the minister teaches both the what and the how of Christian faith. As spiritual leader, the minister counsels the community in its individual and collective growth in faith and self-understanding. As supervising administrator of the life of the community as a whole, the minister is entrusted to exercise timely initiative, patient coaxing, and bold challenge in the various ways the church organizes its life and work. In all these tasks, the minister must function as the primary visionary of the church, keeping alive the animating hope of Christian witness for the benefit of the world. Unless the administering practices of ordained leadership are exercised dynamically and sensitively, the health of the church's life suffers and its capacity for faithful, effective witness is impaired.

The minister must function as the primary visionary of the church, keeping alive the animating hope of Christian witness.

In sum, the ordained leadership leads best by serving—serving first the Lord Jesus Christ and his Gospel and thus too serving the church in its witness to the Gospel. Ministers are accountable to God and to the whole *laos* of the church for the performance of their obligations. They are not to regard themselves as the Head of the church but as servants of Jesus Christ.

Ordained ministers are not the only leaders called out and necessary for the administering of the church's life. The Holy Spirit from time to time calls forth others of the *laos* to whom the church entrusts short-term and long-term tasks and functions for the sake of the church's witness. Such persons—among them those Disciples at present call elders and deacons—engage in practices of providing-servant-leadership which are signs of church's faithfulness to its calling. The distinction between the formally ordained leaders and the non-ordained but called leaders, should remain fluid, open, and nonhierarchical.

The church must remember that its administrative arrangements are not eternal. They are subject to continuous review and reform in light of their conformity with the distinctive social character and distinctive calling of the church amid "the needs and patterns of a changing world" (*Design*, ¶2).

In this third part we have pointed to the defining signs of the church's identity, nature, and purpose—to the best of our understanding. In doing so, we have been able to do something else as well: we have brought to light why, because of our faith in the Gospel the life of the church involves such things as worship, preaching and the sacraments, education, evangelism, confessing the faith, works of compassion, involvement in social action, and ordination. These are so commonplace in church life that even Christians—perhaps Christians especially—are liable to forget or mistake their real meaning. We understand them rightly when we understand their proper connection to the church's God-given identity.

Here, then, we have affirmed that the church is itself a liberative and redemptive communal reality, a gift and calling of God to the world. As the community of the faithful engages in the practices of nurture, outreach, and administration which witness to the living triune God for the sake of the world, it becomes what God has called it to be—truly the church of Jesus Christ.

PART 4

Issues of Relationship and Structure

We have now explained that the church is a community called forth by the Gospel. We have pointed out the defining signs of that community's true identity. One other important topic demands attention—the polity of the church. We are concerned here with issues of relationship and structure. We discuss these issues first in quite general terms. This puts them in proper context, as issues facing the church itself. We then turn to the Disciples specifically, suggesting a number of principles for aligning our relationships and structures in accord with the church's true identity.

Church Organization and Practices of the Church's True Identity

The word "polity" refers to the structuring which makes the community of faith also and at the same time a distinct social grouping that is readily identifiable as a society, an organization, an institution. (Synonyms for polity are similarly shorthand terms such as the structure, the government, and the order or ordering of the church.) This topic is important for many reasons. One is that because the church is not simply a group of people but an organized group—one institution among others—in any given culture, it is a matter of some special concern to the powers and principalities of this world: they are eager to decide for themselves whether to ignore, tolerate, persecute, manipulate, or support it. Another is that these "worldly" attempts to define the church and assign it to a place in the social order of their own choosing often induce Christians to forget the church's true identity.

But the topic is also important because Christians themselves are so divided about church polity, and by their church polities. Is this much ado about nothing? Some say it is. Some say it is not. An adequate answer requires us to examine the question more carefully.

From a strictly social-scientific perspective, church polity is simply another example of "the sociology of organizations." Institutional structuring involves the development of various more or less formalized, routine, and persisting patterns of human interrelations and activities within any given community. Once in place, these patterns facilitate, shape, and place certain restraints on relationships and interactions among the community's members. Taken together as a complex whole, the community's structure of governance, maintenance, and operation also "typifies" its shared life in the sense that it becomes a visible symbol or emblem of the community itself. So far as the sociology of organizations is concerned, it is neither surprising nor troubling that different communities of Christians develop different polities and that each of them then advertises itself as a "Christian Church."

Only rarely do Christians view the issue of church polity with such cool detachment, or feel it right to do so. The sociological viewpoint is certainly true so far as it goes: like clubs and many other forms of human association, communities and community-forming movements of Christians, including the Stone-Campbell movement, are historical examples of what the sociologists call "institutionalization." Yet this account does not by itself provide the answers to the questions of Christian faith with regard to church polity. We must seek to understand how (if at all) church polity has to do with the expression of the church's God-given identity.

The first thing to be said is that we have to deal not only with differing opinions about church polity but with very different experiences of it and very strong feelings about it. There is an inclination, on the one hand, to identify the church itself—the one body which is the body of Christ—with some one specific organizational structure. And there is a tendency, on the other hand, to view what is called the "organized" or "institutional" church with some disdain, as though institutional structure itself were incompatible with the shared life of true Christian community. Both tendencies are found among Disciples, as they are within churches and the public at large. Neither of them, however, reflects a proper understanding of the relationship between the church's true identity and its polity. Nor will it do simply to say that God calls the church to be a half-and-half mixture of community and institution. We must speak instead of a dialectical connection between the two.

Why does the church have to have a "structure"?

In order to grasp this point, it may be helpful to consider the rationale for church polity. Why does the church have to have a "structure" that makes it not only a community with distinctive practices but an organization, an institution?

Because the Gospel calls forth the church, that is, one body whose many members pursue one calling, the shared life of that body finds its living reality in more than heartfelt sentiment alone. Christians are drawn together by faith into a community with historically concrete social form. This is because those faithful to the Gospel cannot be content with occasional, random moments of true community and true ministry; by its very nature faith presses us on to fashion a shared life capable of long-term commitments to one another and to service to God and the neighbor. Only by means of structures is it possible for such a community to maintain from one moment to another—that is, over time—the distinctive social character which makes it a fitting sign of the Gospel and to equip its many members for the practices of nurture and outreach which make it an instrument of God's work of reconciliation. Thus the development of institutional structures which typify even as they facilitate, shape, and place certain restraints upon human relationships is not merely sociologically predictable: it is a natural and necessary outgrowth of faith itself.

To point out the necessity of a church polity is not to argue for the necessity, and hence the sole legitimacy, of any one particular form of polity. This disclaimer is basically the same as the one already made while discussing the administrative practices of the church. But it deserves repeating, considering how often our love for *the* church leads Christians to make sincere yet extravagant claims on behalf of *our own* church's polity. There is a logic to this reasoning: if the church's identity is a gift and calling from God, and if institutional structures are necessary, then there must be one true structure or polity given by God.

This logic is understandable, but not compelling. Institutional structure is not an end in itself or even one end among others; the necessity of church polity is only that of a *means* to another end. The end is that of keeping the church faithful to its God-given identity and mission. In Protestant tradition, this point has often been made by stating that the structure of the church—that is, an institutionalized ordering of the community for ministry—is a matter not of the very being (the *esse*) but the well-being (the *bene esse*) of the church.

Hence the highest praise that can be given to any specific church polity is that it serves its intended purpose well. This judgment, of course, rests ultimately with God. Yet Christians here and now cannot avoid making proximal appraisals of our own in this regard. The church must devise structures of administrative practices (governance, maintenance, and operation) which will promote its well-being in the sense of enabling it to be faithful to its God-given calling in its particular setting in history.

The result of these human devisings is well-known. Churches have developed many different forms of polity in the course of church history. The New Testament itself shows that basic elements of the most prominent forms of polity—congregational, presbyterial or associational, and episcopal—arose so very early in church life that advocates of each speak of its apostolic origins. Variations on these forms, including the distinctive mixed polity of covenant adopted by Disciples in 1968, have emerged as Christians sought to form or reform existing structures by realigning relations among these primary social units of community life. A brief, if over-simple, sketch of how this works out may be helpful.

The church must devise structures which enable it to be faithful to its calling in its particular setting in history.

The living reality of shared life in Christ emerges and is sustained in concrete social form as a group of believers who, living near one another, gather together regularly and, through their face-to-face relations and their practices, witness to the Gospel in that place. This local assembly (the congregation) is the social unit highlighted in congregational polities. The living reality of the union—the communion—of several such local gatherings as one body spread out among differing locations is highlighted by the regional and general connections of the sort formed by presbyterial (or associational) and episcopal polities. The need and desire to achieve what is regarded as a proper, effective balance *among* these local, regional, and general units of the church's corporate life have led some churches, including the Disciples, to adopt a form of "mixed" polity. The outcome, to this date in history, is the coexistence of a large number of distinct organized bodies of Christians. The technical term for these is "particular churches"; in everyday discussion they are called simply the churches or denominations.

Insofar as any or every one of the churches exhibits the defining signs of the church's true identity, Christians must say, "here are disciples of Christ, our sisters and brothers in

Christ, churches which are truly church." Yet these divided churches cannot be said to be fully the church. The full scope of the community of Christian faith extends to the inclusion of all disciples of Christ, i.e., to a universality (catholicity) that is worldwide (the *oikumene,* ecumenical). Thus the coexistence of numerous disparate—separated and often competing—churches is a historical development for which no claim to finality can justly be made. Faith sets in motion a quest for a structuring of relations which will permit the shared life of the whole people to manifest its living reality in some concrete social form. This quest is still underway, for despite many ecumenical advances, Christians have not yet envisioned the polity that can be said by common consent (as it must) to serve this purpose well.

The fact that a structure for the visible unity of all Christians is such an elusive goal, and indeed that so many in all of the churches are resistant and many more apathetic to it, is instructive. It reminds us how much remains to be done before the church fulfills its calling and God's work of reconciliation is to be fully realized. It also alerts us to two other aspects of church polity that deserve comment.

First, the polity of each church shapes that church's common life in such a way that its members are reinforced in their conviction that they thereby belong also to the true church of Jesus Christ. The community of Christian faith—notwithstanding its flaws, imperfections, and shortcomings—cannot do otherwise, trusting as it does in the Gospel. The faith that is confessed, the baptism that is administered, the table that is spread, and the ministries that are undertaken by each of the churches are not their own but those of the Universal Church of Jesus Christ.

But this encouragement is not risk-free: it can give rise to the conviction that *only* by belonging to this particular, polity-structured church is there assurance of belonging to the Universal Church of Jesus Christ. One result is all too familiar: each church operates with an institutionalized assumption that whereas "our church" is both truly Christian and truly church, the status of "your church" and "their church" remains for us a more or less open question.

Today, this question rarely hinders different churches from forming friendly, even cooperative associations. But when ecumenism progresses beyond good will, toleration, consultation, and collaboration, all of the churches become very uncomfortable. While each of them is firmly convinced that *it* is truly church, that conviction is not fully shared by the others. The necessity of agreeing, individually and collectively, on some set of institutional features by which to reassure one another of their common identity in Christ causes each and every one to feel somewhat hurt and resentful.

Second, the difficulty of devising a polity adequate to the living reality of the unity of all Christians alerts us to grave concerns—often outright fear—about institutional structuring present within each and every church. Church polity is also church government: it involves forming structures for the community's collective decision-making. The questions of "who gets to decide and how" generate churchwide high anxiety. This is understandable, and not all bad. After all, every Christian should be anxious to see decision-making lead to the right (the most wise, the most faithful) conclusion and therefore anxious also to see that the decision-making process itself is structured and carried out well.

Yet this anxiety exposes a dimension of church life that we dare not ignore. Human relations within the church are also power-relations. In providing a structure for collective decision-making, the polity of the church serves either to contest or to perpetuate (as the case may be) power-relations among the church members which are already set in place both by the impact of outside socio-cultural forces on the community and by the tenor of informal interpersonal dealings within. In short, church polity is also church politics.

And here again Christians have very different views, experiences, and feelings. For some, church politics itself seems to become a primary outlet for Christian service. Others quite frankly wish it would go away. In fact, shared life in a human community—even that of a community dedicated to Christian faith and love—is always "political." Human relations remain power-relations whether or not they are institutionally structured. These power-relations may embody and produce great good as well as great harm.

The Gospel calls Christians to claim and use their power in relating to others, viewing it as a gift from God by which human relations may be altered for the better, in greater accord with God's will for humanity. The polity and politics of the church are to help maintain and reinforce this alteration *for the better* by institutionally structuring it. Only by *means* of polity is the church capable of functioning over time as one body commonly committed to the pursuit of its one calling. Hence the church must make collective decisions about how to carry out the nurturing and outreach practices of witness to the Gospel. It must also make a collective decision about how these and every other collective decision will be made. Thus the point at issue before each and every church is the same: the formation of a structure of governance, maintenance, and operation that befits the true nature and serves the true purpose of the church.

It is not to be thought that any institutional structure for collective decision-making assures the church of faithfulness in ministry or that any of those known to church history is perfect, and so unreformable. Each of the various institutional arrangements set by the polities of the churches displays certain peculiar strengths and peculiar weaknesses. This simply confirms, however, that issues of polity are among the most fateful that churches are called upon to address. Thus in forming or re-forming our church's polity, and in evaluating those of others, conscientious Christians will be mindful that our every decision sends a message about our understanding of—and commitment to—our Christian faith. We will be mindful as well that the power-plays, trade-offs, and quick-fixes, and "politics as usual" are out of keeping with the true identity of the church.

This is to say that issues of church polity are first and finally issues of faith that must be addressed first and finally in light of our understanding of the church's true identity.

A facility for practical, expedient problem-solving—a pragmatic temper like that to which Disciples justly lay claim to some fame—is of value to the church. Yet it carries Christians only so far. Its appropriate but quite restricted role to play is that of helping the church pursue its calling effectively while setting aside the distractions of other, and lesser things. And its success or failure is to be judged not by how well it enables the church to survive, get by, or even grow in numbers by market appeal, but by how well it contributes to the fulfillment of the church's God-given calling to witness to God's love for the sake of the world.

Having been joined in one body and entrusted with one ministry by God, the church bears responsibility for collective theological judgments regarding its practices of witness to God's redemptive love for the world. These are in no sense blind or arbitrary judgments: they are guided by the light of Scripture, informed by the traditions and experiences of the Church Universal, and responsive to the needs of a suffering, strife-torn world. In its efforts to understand and evaluate these resources wisely and well, the church is aided by what Disciples customarily term "diversity of theological opinion" among its members.

It is through the interdependence, interaction, and complementarity of diverse theological viewpoints that the community fulfills its calling to "be of one mind." This diversity is also essential for the goal of growing in our understanding of the faith and that of upbuilding the whole. Indeed, a basic Christian conviction is that no person, group, or church possesses a full grasp of the will of God. Even as we strive to live according to God's self-revelation in Jesus Christ, we continue to see "in a mirror, dimly" (1 Corinthians 13:12), interpreting the Scriptures, the heritage of the church, and our own experience of God's presence and promise in remarkably different ways. This multiplicity of theological view is characteristic of the Scriptures themselves which, to cite only one example, contain not one Gospel account but four. The proper conclusion to draw from this is that the church needs various viewpoints in order to hear the Gospel more clearly and to understand its meaning more fully.

It follows that as in its practices of education and its practices of evangelism, so too in the polity which links together all of its administrative practices, the church has to be a community of dialogue—sustained, churchwide conversation about God, the Gospel, and our participation in the work of God. This dialogue is not only an acknowledgement but a sharing together of the rich meaning of faith, and so an expression of living communion and a witness to the Gospel. Without such dialogue, the smooth running of the church becomes merely mechanistic, its unity becomes merely formal, and its diversity becomes self-indulgent and contentious.

When we engage in genuine dialogue, we come willing to both teach and learn. We commit ourselves to listen carefully to one another, refusing to vaunt ourselves or caricature others. We commit ourselves as well to enter into conversation as informed as possible of the multifaceted Christian heritage, and we expect that we and our conversation partners alike will come away even better informed, having deepened and broadened and perhaps corrected our initial views in light of the dialogue itself. Dialogue of this sort is by no means, then, a zero-sum game whereby the affirmation of one participant means the automatic rejection of others. Indeed, the point is not "winning" at all. It is to discern more clearly and fully what God wills for the life of the church and each of its members. And on the basis of this process of discernment, the church equips itself for the ministry to which God has called it.

Disciples Polity: Always Reforming

Reflections on the polity of the Christian Church (Disciples of Christ) are to be guided and ruled by our best understanding of the church's true identity, nature, and purpose. Our *Design* reformed our church's organizational life. It affirms that ours is a community formed by covenant relationship with God and one another. In keeping with that covenant, God's covenant of love in Jesus Christ, we restructured our life together in Christ along the lines of a covenantal polity. Hence each of the challenges and questions we face today brings with it another question as well: is our church structure capable of serving its intended purpose?

Ours is a community formed by covenant relationship with God and one another.

This question calls for more than a simple yes or no answer, and more too than ad hoc responses to institutional emergencies. It requires evaluating the total structure of the church in light of the character and obligations of our covenantal calling. This reevaluation, we believe, is to be of paramount concern to Disciples in response to what are perceived as stresses, strains, and shortcomings of our church structure. Neither maintaining nor altering that structure can be finally justified on any other basis. Thus the concern is not only paramount but urgent, and deserves churchwide attention.

Discussions about organizational change are already underway within our church. Others will surely follow, and in due course action will be proposed and taken. From all that has been said of the church's true identity, there emerge a number of points which merit attention during this period of churchwide deliberation.

1. The covenant conception of church set out in the Preamble of the *Design* is an apt expression for the foundation, nature, and purpose of the church. The particularities of organizational structure set forth in the *Design*, however, are properly viewed as the timely means by which our life-in-covenant with God and one another was given an institutional embodiment in "earthen vessels." Timely as they were, and surely in many instances still of value, those means are of human design and therefore reformable. The *Design* is open to amendment, and in any case allows considerable latitude and flexibility for realigning our church's structural units, relations, policies, and projects. Yet neither the desire nor the

pressure to reform the organizational structures of our church should blind us to significant, hard-won gains made by the adoption of the *Design*. Among the gains that are too precious ever to be "reformed" away, even in the name of dire practical necessity, are these:

- that God's covenant of love in Jesus Christ is the prior and final reality of our lives;
- that this covenant draws us into covenant community one with another;
- that the covenant community into which we are drawn is the church, and hence one body which, through sacred vows of union in local (congregational), regional, and general spheres of association, participates in the Church universal;
- that the character and activity of this community are to be fitting witnesses to the Gospel of Jesus Christ, for the benefit of the world, to the glory of God.

Acknowledgements such as these are standards to be used in evaluating proposals for the maintenance or the alteration of our church structure. In adapting organizational forms and relationships, care must be taken that we reinforce, not weaken, the covenantal ties which bind us to God and one another.

2. In addition to these acknowledgements, other concerns of covenantal faithfulness ought not to be overlooked in dealing with issues of church structure. One is a lesson we learn from Scripture, the Disciples heritage of checks-and-balances among power centers, and the experiences of women and minorities. Organizational structures have the power to liberate or to alienate. We should therefore examine church structure in order to determine when, where, and who it liberates and when, where, and who it alienates. And we should seek those structures which empower every member of the body as well as the body as a whole for ministry.

   Another, equally important lesson has to do with maintaining a finely balanced, creative tension between tradition and innovation. Each has value. A church that hastily jettisons tradition will be easy prey to fads and demagoguery. A church that is too resistant to change risks failing to heed the Holy Spirit which, speaking through the cries of those outside established circles of power and privilege or through the still, small voice of conscience within, directs us beyond the status quo. Therefore, examine church structure in light of its capacity to discern those elements of tradition worth preserving and those innovations worth accepting. And seek structures that conserve the best of the church's heritage while allowing for fresh insights and new initiatives.

Structures of this sort value inclusivity, diversity, tolerance, and flexibility. They aim at maintaining a balanced, creative tension between the power of the individual/congregation and the group/church. Whatever decisions are finally made must be subject to appeal and reconsideration, and conscientious dissent must be allowed. Yet on occasion the church must take a clear stand, and once taken, firmly held—until with greater wisdom we are shown a still more perfect way. All those we entrust with leadership and decision-making authority in the church are fallible. Blind obedience and servile submission to others have no place in covenant community. But each of us is fallible too, no less so than the covenant partners to whom we have entrusted leadership and decision-making authority. Unyielding insistence on having our own way and withdrawing from or inflicting pain on our brothers and sisters when we disagree with them are breaches of our covenantal promises.

3. The evaluation and adaptation of church structures in keeping with our covenantal obligations are matters of judgment which call for wise collective decision-making. Hence it is imperative that we structure and conduct the process of collective decision-making in our church in a manner befitting a covenant community. The voices of all in the church are to be heard. Each member and each group needs opportunity to share in shaping the

life and work of the church. Because it is impossible for all Christians to gather together to make every decision, even in our congregations, the church is well-advised to rely on methods of representative self-government, and to embrace basic democratic values which honor open, reasoned debate, respect the will of the majority and the integrity of the minority, and invite the common consent of all. This is certainly a part of what it means to live and serve in covenant together.

4. The collegial decisions that Disciples make are decisions about whether and how we will be the church. These are decisions regarding our understanding of the Christian faith we share as a covenant community, and so—as the word theology refers to "faith seeking understanding"—they are theological decisions. Collegial theological decisions are made constantly, and routinely, by the community of faith, among Disciples within and across the local, regional, and general manifestations of our church. Many of these decisions are by now so much part of our own church tradition—for example, "as Disciples, our congregation celebrates the Lord's Supper every Sunday, and this is what we say and do"—that we are hardly aware that they are indeed collective and theological and decisions. The same holds for the many decisions customarily thought of as simply practical, or perhaps even "worldly." It is common, for example, to hear it said that our church assemblies deal, or should deal, only with items of "business" rather than of "theology"—as if the teaching of the faith were not the business of the church and the business of the church (including the stewardship of funds) were not bound up with our understanding of the church's faith.

To these examples of the collective theological decisions we make, many others can be added. It is unfortunate when such decisions in the church go unrecognized for what they really are, and even more so when they are made without benefit of the wide-ranging, open, and earnest theological dialogue that they deserve. Disciples are by no means to be singled out in this respect. There is no foolproof system of church self-government, and given the persisting power of sin among Christians, none is to be expected. For its part, the structure of our church provides for collective decision making in the manner of a demographically inclusive representative democracy. There is nothing in or about that structure to prevent us from engaging in theological dialogue and in theologically deliberative decision making. We need only to resolve to do so.

Disciples certainly have good reason to keep close watch over church decision making and its outcomes.

Disciples, like Christians in every church, certainly have good reason to keep close watch over church decision making and its outcomes. We want the process to be fair, and its outcomes, wise. Theological opinion in our church is certainly varied—so much so that the popular image of a single spectrum of positions ranging from conservative to liberal or from traditional to innovative is doomed to misrepresent it. By its heritage and ethos, our church commends freedom, inclusiveness, openness, tolerance, non-judgmentalism, and anti-authoritarianism. These qualities of shared life as church are in keeping with the gift and claim of the Gospel, which is a message of reconciliation, liberation, and redemption. They are in fact to be counted among the *theological* strengths of our church, regardless of their public appeal at any given moment in history. Insistence on uniformity in every detail of church teaching and practice (creedalism, dogmatism, ecclesiasticism, and parochialism) is always a clear and present danger to the church. Equally dangerous, however, is an attitude of laxity or indifferentism which says that "anything goes" and that "diversity of opinion" knows no bounds—in short, that faith and faithfulness amount to whatever any individual or group chooses to make of them.

5. It is therefore incumbent upon congregations, regions, and general units of our church to encourage theological dialogue and to exemplify the value of careful theological deliberation by the way decisions are made and their outcomes are reported. Above all, members of our church need to be equipped as well as encouraged to take on the theological responsibility which falls to us because our church seeks a structure along the lines of a representative democracy. It would therefore be well for Disciples to assess whether our organizational structure makes sufficient provision for channeling our diversity of theological viewpoints along paths leading to the upbuilding of the whole body. Over the years efforts have been made, some quite fruitful, to help our church become a community of theological conversation—through, e.g., churchwide conferences, study commissions, and workshops at assemblies. Even so, occasional efforts are no substitute for the formation of organizational structures promoting study, reflection, dialogue, and constructive debate about issues of faith and the meaning of faithfulness throughout the church.

   In this regard, there is need for Disciples to clarify when and how our church might best express its corporate judgment on basic issues of faith. People wish and in any case deserve to know the beliefs and practices that are upheld by the Christian Church (Disciples of Christ). Faithfulness to the Gospel and effectiveness in ministry demand clarity on this matter. This need is as critical to congregational life and to regions as it is to the general church. But precisely because it is general, the general church—especially the General Assembly—is the high-profile, churchwide arena in which we demonstrate our unity and our disunity. It is important, then, that Disciples clarify the role of the General Assembly (as well as the general administrative units and their officers) in discerning and expressing the common teachings of our church. It is likewise important to specify the theological bases and implications of what our *Design* refers to as the nature, purpose, functions, rights, and responsibilities of the general, regional, and congregational manifestations of our church.

6. As these comments indicate, to speak of the collective theological decisions of the church is not to speak of any one individual or group legislating and then trying to enforce a uniform understanding of the meaning of faith throughout the church. It is to say, instead, that the church as a whole is responsible for providing means, through its structure, for making collective theological decisions about the teachings and practices of our church. Our covenant conception of church requires that in devising these means we acknowledge that congregations, regions, and general units function as inseparable, interdependent, and complementary parts of the one body. It also requires that whenever collective decisions are made, we carefully distinguish between those truly "essential" matters which the Gospel obliges (or forbids) us to affirm and those "non-essentials" on which wide diversity of thought and practice is embraced within the life of our church.

   This wording calls to mind a maxim that Disciples long ago incorporated into our heritage: "In essentials unity; in non-essentials, liberty; in all things, charity." Although neither strictly biblical nor especially trendy, it is wise counsel nonetheless. As Disciples, we can learn from the course our journey in faith has taken that it is wise counsel with too little practical effect unless and until it finds its way into our church's decision-making and other organizational structures. The only truly timely, and truly faithful, means by which to give our life-in-covenant with God and one another proper institutional embodiment in these times will be those which make this maxim the guideline for every undertaking of the Christian Church (Disciples of Christ).

In concluding we must emphasize a point that has been allowed to remain in the background throughout: namely, the church witnesses to God for the benefit of the world to the glory of God. In a distinctively Christian sense, the world's true benefit, and therefore also its glory, is first and last prefigured and contained in God's glory. The glory of God that the church knows in Jesus Christ is a glory which includes the glory of the world of sinners reconciled, liberated, and redeemed. God's glory is not God's selfish possession; it is a glory shared with the world by the One God—Creator, Redeemer, and Sustainer of all things. Hence, it is not necessarily a glory on the world's terms, nor is it always a *benefit* on the world's terms. But God's glory is the only truly eternal benefit for the world. The church is true to its identity when it witnesses to the glory of God as the reality from which and towards which all things move.

PART 5

Reports to the General Assembly

A Word to the Church on Ecclesiology (1979)

The Commission on Theology and Christian Unity, authorized by the General Board and implemented by the Council on Christian Unity, has held two meetings—one in October 1978 and the second in June 1979. Given its focus upon the general topic of ecclesiology, or the nature of the Church, the Commission devoted its second meeting to a detailed analysis and evaluation of *The Design of the Christian Church (Disciples of Christ).*Papers presented for and presented to the Commission are as follows:

"An Ecclesiological Inventory" by James O. Duke

"Theological Issues in the Restructure of the Christian Church (Disciples of Christ)" by Ronald E. Osborn

"A Theological Analysis of *The Design*" by Joe R. Jones

"Decision-Making and Zones of Conflict in the Christian Church (Disciples of Christ)" by Howard Goodrich, Jr.

"Covenant, Local Church, and Universal Church," by Wallace R. Ford

"Gospel and Witness" by Kenneth E. Henry

From the onset of the Commission's deliberations, we rediscovered solid, indeed unanimous agreement that *The Design* is a remarkable achievement and calls attention to the progress Disciples made in the 1960s as they thought and lived their way toward a self-understanding about the nature and structure of the Church. While *The Design* signals a major achievement, it nevertheless is recognized to be a document in process even though it is no longer provisional. A number of theological issues need further exploration and refinement, or so it seems to the Commission. Without attempting to be comprehensive, we have identified the following areas of strategic concern:

I. Manifestations of the Church

The concept of three manifestations of the Church (congregational, regional and general) is unique and one of the strengths of *The Design.* This fuller understanding of the reality of Church is a considerable step forward in the Disciples tradition.

The Commission intends to do further study and reflection on the question of the interrelationship among the different manifestations. Two questions deserve special consideration. (1) Do the manifestations require each other for their own integrity and proper work, or do their free and voluntary relationships make them self-sufficient? (2) If they do require each other, in what ways should they interact? We perceive that an ambivalence continues to exist between the convenantal theme and the emphasis on free and voluntary relationships.

Attention also has been given to the role of the regional minister. Does the tendency toward larger and fewer regions put pressure on regional ministers to perform solely as administrators at the expense of their prophetic ministry and their desire to serve as pastors within the regional manifestation?

In a number of places *The Design* (e.g., paragraph 2) says the church is to "manifest itself" in different ways. The Commission is concerned to stress that the church in all its manifestations is called into being by God. The language of *The Design* tends to obscure God's initiative in creating the people of God.

II. Covenant

The Commission on Theology and Christian Unity observes the way the concept of covenant is explicitly stated in *The Design* and the way it appears to be implicit throughout. Fundamental to the concept of covenant is the acknowledgment of God's call of his people into community under the Lordship of Christ. Only that acknowledgment allows us to speak of ourselves as church.

In the period since Disciples approved *The Design* (initially *The Provisional Design*), the Commission observes that there has increasingly been acceptance and use of the concept of covenant. An exploration of the theological implications of covenant has prompted the Commission to raise several questions:

Are Disciples giving sufficient attention to the role of Divine initiative in covenant?

Have we conceived of covenant unilaterally as *our* initiative without regard to the divine call?

Do disciples tend to employ "covenant" in too limited a fashion, e.g., as implying loyalty to our present structures? Do disciples tend to understand covenant as contractual rather than relational?

Do Disciples see the covenantal implication of Baptism and the Lord's Supper?

Does our concept of sacraments as covenantal relate us explicitly to the suffering and the oppressed?

III. The Affirmation of Faith

The Commission on Theology and Christian Unity gave careful attention to the meaning and status of the first paragraph of the "Preamble" of *The Design.* This paragraph is strongly Christocentric and universal, emphasizing the Lordship of Christ over the Church and the world, and stressing the mission of the Church to all people. In language which is irenic and liturgical in character, the paragraph accentuates the various experiences of the church. It does not, however, include the classical reciting of the mighty acts of God, an important part of affirming the Christian faith. Further, the paragraph does not mention either sin or the forgiveness of sin; it also needs to be strengthened at the point of eschatology. The status of the paragraph is also deliberately not stated in *The Design*. It clearly is not a test of faith, but it seems close to traditional confessions or affirmations of faith.

Obviously the question of the meaning and use of this first paragraph requires further discussion and evaluation. The Commission invites responses concerning the content and the use of this "affirmation of faith" in the church's worship, proclamation, and nurture.

IV. Other Issues

In addition to the concept of manifestations, the idea of covenant and the affirmation of faith, other issues have surfaced in the Commission's first two sessions and will be placed on the agenda of subsequent meetings. We believe these are central themes for a viable Disciples concept of the Church. An outline of themes proposed for study and discussion at our future meetings include

1980—*The Church and Its Witness* (sub-themes: "Church Membership and Belonging," "Church Unity and the Gospel," "The Church's Relationship to the World," and "Evangelism and Liberation")

1981—*Authority* (sub-themes: "Biblical Authority," "The Place of Tradition," "The Nature of the Covenant," and "Decision-Making: The Politics of Authority")

1982—*Ministry* (sub-themes: "Ordination," "Episcope," "Eldership and Diaconate and the Ministry of the Laity")

1983—*Sacraments* (sub-themes: "Sacramental Understanding Among Disciples," "Baptism," "The Lord's Supper," and "Worship")

In preparation for each of these studies attention will be given to seeking a liaison relationship between the Commission and others in our structures who are working on these themes and issues to be addressed. In each of these phases or themes we will seek for a degree of understanding of the Church's unity. The themes of ecclesiology and unity will provide the overall context for the six-year period of study. Only with such a commitment can the Commission help Disciples to develop a more adequate theological interpretation of the Christian Church (Disciples of Christ) and help all of us to discover a greater self-understanding and identity of Disciples *in via* toward witness and service in the world today—and in the future.

V. Sharing with the Church: A Specific Project

Since we believe the papers and issues from our first two meetings would provide fruitful study and reflection for the whole church, we intend to seek the services of the Christian Board of Publication and other units to publish as soon as possible a small study book which would include the major papers, with a study guide. We hope this study would be undertaken by ministers and elders and other leadership groups, e.g., clusters of ministers, boards of elders, regional boards, etc. Such a booklet would stimulate thoughtful study on the nature and mission of the church, as well as *The Design* and other issues which have surfaced among our people in the past decade.

VI. Conclusion

We thank the church for the task given the Commission on Theology and Christian Unity. We find it challenging, demanding, and fulfilling. We believe, more than ever, this dialogue has major importance for the present life and future destiny of the Christian Church (Disciples of Christ).

Members of the Commission on Theology

William R. Baird
Walter D. Bingham
Eugene W. Brice
Paul A. Crow, Jr.
James O. Duke
Arla J. Elston
Wallace R. Ford
H. Jackson Forstman
Thomas Fountain
Clark M. Williamson
Howard Goodrich, Jr.
Ronald W. Graham
Kenneth Henry
Joe R. Jones
Vance Martin
Ronald E. Osborn
Albert M. Pennybacker
Narka Ryan
Robert A. Thomas
William E. Tucker
Ann Uppdegraff
Robert K. Welsh (*staff*)

Questions for Reflection and Discussion

1. Note the questions raised by the commission in 1979 in section II, "Covenant." Which questions remain appropriate to ask today? If the questions are appropriate to ask today, does it suggest any pressing Disciples "agenda" that remains unfinished?
2. Does your faith community make use of the Preamble to the *Design of the Christian Church (Disciples of Christ)* as an affirmation of faith in worship? How do you respond to the critical observations offered by the commission in Section III? Why are such questions important for every faith community to periodically ask?

A Word to the Church on Church on Witness, Mission, and Unity (1981)

The Commission on Theology and Christian Unity, authorized by the General Board and implemented through the Council on Christian Unity, has held three meetings so far: October 6–8, 1978; June 1–3, 1979; and the third on August 29–31, 1980. The general theme for the Commission's work during this six-year mandate is to examine and explore issues related to the nature of the Church for Disciples.

At its third (1980) session, the Commission devoted itself to study of the theme "The Church as a Witnessing Community." The major paper for this meeting, which was prepared by Dr. T. J. Liggett, President, Christian Theological Seminary, focused upon "The Biblical and Theological Perspectives on the Nature of the Church as an Agent for Mission." Sub-themes were introduced by Dr. Paul A. Crow, Jr., President, Council on Christian Unity, on "Unity and the New Context for Witness"; the Rev. Rhodes Thompson, Jr., pastor, Memorial Boulevard Christian Church in St. Louis, on "The Missionary Character of the Congregation"; and Dr. Robert A. Thomas, President, Division of Overseas Ministries, on "Towards a Theology of Mission, General Principles and Policies of the Division of Overseas Ministries of the Christian Church (Disciples of Christ)."

The discussion during the meeting was most lively, and at points the debate illustrated a genuine difference of perspective among members of the Commission as we sought to define what it means for the Church to witness today. Our focus was not only upon the Church, but also the world. We became increasingly aware of the difficulty of speaking about the Church's witness unless, and until, we had also struggled with the context of the world, whose conditions the Gospel addresses and whose voices cry out from situations of starvation, oppression, injustice, and fear. We discovered again the truth that a fragmented Church cannot engage effectively in mission: a divided church simply cannot truly speak God's word of reconciliation to a warring and broken world.

It became clear to the Commission that the context of our discussions could not—indeed must not—be set in any other context than *whole* Gospel, *whole* church, and *whole* world. And each of these dimensions opens for us both exciting possibilities and meanings, and at the same time, enormous challenges and responsibilities.

We wrestled both with the Scriptures and with our present situation to discover the meaning of the Church as a witnessing community in our time. This "Word to the Church" is an invitation to all Disciples to join in this dialogue—a dialogue between faith affirmations and faith questions, between the Gospel and the world, between the church which we are and the church which God calls us to be. We believe this dialogue requires all manifestations of our church to take seriously the contemporary calling to witness, mission and unity.

Affirmation on the Nature of Witness, Mission, and Unity

1. We affirm that the mission of the Church is to witness to God in the world.

Commentary: In the New Testament the creation of the Church is understood to be a part of God's purpose in continuing the ministry of Jesus Christ through the power of the Holy Spirit. The existence of the Church itself is part of the essence of God's mission. The Church, the *ecclesia*, is the community of persons "summoned for a particular purpose." And that purpose is of God—a mission which transcends the Church and for which the Church was brought into being. The Church is thus an agent for God's mission in the world.

2. We affirm that God has "called the Church into being"—but, this calling does not guarantee (1) evidence of any merit on our part; (2) assurance of a privileged position in his Kingdom; (3) special access to God's grace; or (4) any exemption from God's judgment. The calling is to witness to God's purposes of the redemption of the whole of history and the whole of creation.

Commentary: The Church is essentially called into being by the revelation of God in Jesus Christ. It is God who has chosen. "But you are a chosen race, a royal priesthood, a holy nation, God's own people, that you may declare the wonderful deeds of him who called you out of darkness into his marvelous light. Once you were no people but now you are God's people; once you had not received mercy but now you have received mercy." (I Peter 2:9–10)

And, as Paul proclaimed: "Therefore, if anyone is in Christ, he is a new creation; the old has passed away; behold, the new has come. All this is from God, who through Christ reconciled us to himself and gave us the ministry of reconciliation...So we are ambassadors of Christ, God making his appeal through us." (II Cor. 5:17,18, 20)

The calling of the eternal God in its truest and highest sense is a calling to mission: to join with God in his purpose to redeem the whole of humankind, to overcome alienation, to free all persons from bondage and oppression, and to restore harmony to his creation.

3. We affirm that mission is centered in a faithful witness to the Kingdom of God—looking both to our present situation (where God is already at work) and to the future Kingdom (where all will be fulfilled). Mission thus reflects our trust both in the present signs of the Kingdom and in its future culmination. We do not usher in the Kingdom by our actions or activity; rather we seek faithfully to reflect the coming Kingdom in our present life and relationships.

Commentary: However real the evil of the world may be—and it is real; however great the rebellion of humanity may be against God—and it is great; however stark may be the disobedience of human beings—and it is undesirable; the Bible affirms that some way and someday, the will of the Creator God will ultimately prevail and the kingdoms of this world will truly be the Kingdom of God in which His will is done on earth as it is in heaven. The author of Ephesians has expressed this understanding in the following words: "For he has made known to us in all wisdom and insight the mystery of his will, according to his purpose which he set forth in Christ as a plan for the fullness of time, to unite all things in him, things in heaven and things on earth." (Eph.1:9, 10)

This vision of God's will and Kingdom, something which is already present, but also coming in splendor—this is the point of reference of the life and mission of the *ecclesia*.

4. We affirm that the Good News of Jesus Christ embraces all people, though its announcement is received in differing ways. This Gospel is experienced as a two-edged sword. For example, to some it speaks a word of hope and freedom; to others it speaks a word of judgment. However, in each situation and to all people it is the same Gospel being announced and proclaimed.

Commentary: The announcement of the Gospel of Jesus Christ comes to all persons. It comes to the poor, and in them it often generates the power to affirm their human dignity, liberation, and hope. It comes to the rich, and in them it often speaks a word of judgment, challenge, and a call to repentance. To the insensitive, it comes as a call to awareness of responsibility. The Gospel is "good news" to all who trust in God rather than the power of the world, to all who "do good." "There will be tribulation and distress for every human who does evil...but glory and honor and peace for every one who does good...For God shows no partiality." (Romans 2:9–11)

5. We affirm that witness requires unity among Christians. Church division denies faithful witness to God and weakens the resources for mission in the world.

Commentary: The Church of Christ is one. All persons who confess faith in Jesus as Lord are part of the one body. The divisions which historical, geographical, sociological, theological, and liturgical factors produce are limitations upon the proper functioning of the Body. The world is too strong for a divided church. In a world where ignorance of the Gospel and desperate human need and oppression are so massive, neither a single denomination nor any national tradition can carry out the global mission. Faithful witness to the Gospel requires unity among Christians. Commitment to evangelism, mission, and justice is inseparable from a commitment to church union.

6. We affirm that a new vision of the Church is needed for effective witness today—a vision which sees the Church as a community of God's love in and to the world and thus becomes an agent for mission, offering servant leadership, and looking to the unity of humankind.

Commentary: To perceive that the Church is essentially a community of God's love, serving as an "agent for mission," makes it clear that a new vision of "church" is desperately needed—a vision which gives primacy to the missionary character of the people God has called to be his witnesses. Trial vision will determine its structures, guide in its selection of leadership, and shape its inner life, with love of God and neighbor as its point of reference. "We love, because he first loved us. If anyone says, 'I love God,' and hates his brother, he is a liar; for he who does not love his brother whom he has seen, cannot love God whom he has not seen." (I John 4:19–20)

This vision is based upon God's revelation in Christ Jesus. Its mission is neither self-initiated, nor self-serving; rather the Church is to be a servant and is called to servant leadership and agenda. Servanthood calls us out of self, out of exclusiveness and selfishness into the universal horizon of the unity of all humankind. The Church is called to live from and toward that unity.

7. We affirm that witness involves Christian discipline and growth in spirituality. But these are not to be interpreted as a new ethic of religious laws, or as excessive concern for one's own state of being. Both discipline and spirituality are marked by the concern to bring together word and deed, proclamation and performance.

Commentary: Discipline and spirituality are integral to faithful Christian witness. We do not understand discipline to mean the restoring of a rigid perfectionism based upon legal requirements. Rather, we look to that character of the Christian life which seeks always to bridge the gap of faith and action, of what we say and what we do. Spirituality has too often been focused solely upon an introspective and unhealthy concern for our own well-being, happiness, security, or standing. Spirituality is—or should be—that quality of life in the "Spirit" which enables Christians to live out their faith in service and servanthood in the midst of the contemporary world.

Discipline and spirituality are gifts of the faith, not obligations. They are central elements in keeping the vision of the servant church at the forefront of our mission. They serve to enable us to overcome our blindness in seeing that witness is obscured and weakened whenever we stand with lifestyles, as individuals or as churches, which conspicuously contradict the essential message of the Gospel. As Paul wrote in the closing words of his letter to the churches in Galatia: "But God forbid that I should boast of anything but the cross of our Lord Jesus Christ, through which the world is crucified to me and I to the world!...for I bear the marks of Jesus branded upon my body." (Gal. 6:14, 17)

8. We affirm that evangelism is a central aspect of witness. But evangelism is not just a matter of "saving souls" or "church growth." It carries the concerns for developing maturity in the Christian life and faith through commitment to justice, caring, and overcoming alienation, suffering, hopelessness, and oppression in the world. Witness and evangelism seek always to enable persons to live by faith in Jesus Christ as Lord and Savior.

Commentary: The witness of the Church is aimed at making credible that which otherwise might be in doubt—that is, to "enable" faith. The point of reference is clear: the Kingdom of God. The role of the Church is clear: to be a faithful witness. Fidelity in our witness must be an overarching concern of the Church and its leadership. Concern for whether a church is large or small, weak or strong, growing or diminishing, secure or endangered, must never supersede the concern for the fidelity of witness.

The mission of the Church by definition includes evangelism proclaiming and sharing the Good News of God in Jesus Christ. But, we reject as unacceptable the false dichotomy often set forth between evangelism and engagement with problems in society. In this time of new formations and understanding we urge that evangelism not be too narrowly defined. It should not be rooted in institutional survival, expressed solely as membership recruitment, or concerned only for numerical growth.

True evangelism is the proclamation of the Gospel which brings new life. It is proper to be concerned about the numerical growth of the Church through those who bear witness to Jesus Christ as Lord and Savior. But a single emphasis on numerical growth often obscures the need for continued repentance and new life. Evangelism must also be concerned about the growth of maturity in the faith in which individuals deepen their commitment to God and neighbor, and witness in word and deed to God's nature and purpose.

Questions Yet to Be Explored

As the Commission on Theology and Christian Unity shared in dialogue about the nature of the Church's witness, some complex issues arose which need further discussion by Disciples. These questions "yet-to-be-explored" are set forth in the hope that the honesty of our church's exploration and probing would be seen not simply in reaching agreement, but also in identifying areas for reflection upon our church's understanding of the crucial issues of witness, mission, and unity. We share these questions in order to invite discussion and response throughout our whole church.

1. What do we mean by the Kingdom of God?

A primary image which runs throughout our earlier affirmations is that of the Kingdom of God. In our discussions several fundamental issues were raised regarding clarity around this concept which is so central to Christian witness.

First, though we pray "Thy Kingdom come," we do not know precisely what that Kingdom will look like in concrete terms. *How do we view our present world in relation to the Kingdom which is to come? How do we determine if we are witnessing to God's Kingdom and not simply to false kingdoms of human design?*

Second, we became aware of a wide variety of voices which proclaim that they are witnessing to the Kingdom of God. Each of these professes to be speaking for the Christian faith. The voices are many. The question is: *How are we to judge between the voices and their various claims, especially when they seem to be in contradiction with each other, while pointing to the same source in Jesus Christ?*

Third, we know that God is an incarnate God, working in and through human beings and human activities. However, we are also aware that the Gospel can too easily become captured by an ideology. For example, the leaders in Nazi Germany claimed to be acting upon "Christian" beliefs. *How do we keep our witness focused upon God's Kingdom and not upon lesser kingdoms of this world? How do we distinguish between the true Gospel and false gospel in our time?*

2. How do we understand the church's witness in relation to the poor?

Throughout our discussion we identified the Gospel (and the image of God's Kingdom) as experienced by most Christians of the world as a witness to God's solidarity with the poor. Perhaps this is most clearly stated in the proclamation of Jesus: "Blessed are you poor, for yours is the Kingdom of God." (Luke 6:20)

The questions set before us as we struggled to understand God's word for our church today were: *How does our witness include the dimension of living in solidarity with the poor? How do we hear their voices and challenges? What implications does the increasing poverty and oppression in our world have for our church's witness, mission, and unity? What is the Good News of the Gospel for both poor and rich? When, and in what respects, does the Gospel sound like bad news?*

3. What is the meaning of salvation today?

Salvation is a central concept in understanding Christian witness. Some would say that salvation is a matter solely of individual conversion; others express salvation in terms of reordering the structures of society in terms of justice and human dignity. The questions to be explored are: *How do we understand salvation? How does it include both individual and corporate dimensions? How do we understand that both persons and society are called under God's judgment and mercy?*

4. What does it mean to keep the elements of mission and unity together as essential marks of Christian witness?

Too often the concerns for mission are expressed as being over against the concern for Christian unity. Some would say the urgent tasks for the church are related to the world's needs and not to a unity of church organization. But we are also aware that a divided church is not able to speak God's word of reconciliation to a divided world. A united church is required for effective mission. Indeed, unity itself becomes a sign witnessing to God's power at work among his people. The question, therefore, remains: *How do we hold together unity and mission as common expressions of the Church's witness in our world today? How do we perceive the Church as binding us together even in the tension of diversified forms of witness?*

Members of the Commission on Theology

H.Jackson Forstman, *Chair*	Kenneth Henry
William R. Baird	Joe R. Jones
Walter D. Bingham	Vance Martin
Eugene W. Brice	Ronald E. Osborn
Paul A. Crow, Jr.	Albert M. Pennybacker
James O. Duke	Narka Ryan
Aria J. Elston	Robert A. Thomas
Wallace R. Ford	William E. Tucker
Thomas Fountain	Ann Uppdegraff Spleth
Howard Goodrich	Clark M. Williamson
Ronald H. Graham	Robert K. Welsh (*staff*)

Questions for Reflection and Discussion

1. Invite those in your congregation responsible for developing outreach and/or evangelism opportunities to meet with the group. Discuss the "Questions Yet to Be Explored" (pp. 80–82). List your comments on newsprint.
2. Review your responses to the above question. In what ways do these question or challenge the evangelism or outreach work you and/or your faith community are committed to today? Explore together what God may be calling you to do differently or more intentionally to be more empowered by the beliefs underlying the outreach and evangelism you do.

A Word to the Church on Authority (1983)

I. Introduction

As the Commission on Theology and Christian Unity has explored its consideration of the nature of the Church (ecclesiology) for the Christian Church (Disciples of Christ), we have come to focus on the issue of authority. Indeed, the critical place of this issue in any understanding of the church led us to spend two years (1981–1982) in reflecting upon its significance. We have been reminded that throughout Christian history, the church has sought to define and clarify the role of authority, as one of those factors which condition authentic witness to the Gospel. We have also sensed the new urgency about this issue, which is described as "a crisis of authority" which affects our society and the church. Who speaks for God? How does the will of Jesus Christ become contemporary for the church?

These are essential questions—which have to do with authority—for Christians as they witness to a meaningful faith. We hope this paper will move our church to reflect on the meaning of authority.

Our consideration of authority is new terrain for Disciples, and may be the most difficult aspect of ecclesiology for us. Our memory has historic fears of the abuses of authority and power (authoritarianism) in the church. Indeed, our self-image has long been as a church with a healthy suspicion of authoritarianism which our forefathers and mothers in the faith defined as any claim to authority beyond the Bible. But we believe that more is demanded of our church than "healthy suspicion." Authority—distinct from authoritarianism—is a gift of the Gospel.

The Christian Church (Disciples of Christ) has lived for many decades without a clearly defined statement on authority. Our ancient slogans, such as "No Creed but Christ" and "No Book but the Bible," while valuable witnesses, are not full testimonies, and need to be interpreted in light of the contemporary situation. Even in the period of restructure (1960–1968) we did not fully come to grips, pragmatically or theologically, with the issues related to authority in the church. But this issue, we believe, requires our serious consideration. A church which is unwilling to search for a common understanding of Christian authority will be controlled by biblicism, self-seeking individuals, or self-serving institutions.

In light of this history of hesitancy, a legitimate question which might be addressed to the Commission on Theology and Christian Unity is: Why should we address the issue of authority now? Three answers can be given, all of which place this issue centrally on our agenda in the coming years:

(a) We are living in a time when Disciples, along with other churches, increasingly need to speak with authority on critical issues confronting Christians in a complex and pluralistic society.

(b) A theology of the church requires us to wrestle with such questions as, How does the Church teach authoritatively today? In what ways can a church make corporate decisions on issues of faith and ethics which can be claimed as an important part of Christian witness?

(c) The wider ecumenical discussions—COCU's "emerging theological consensus"; the WCC's convergence statement on *Baptism, Eucharist, and Ministry*; and dialog with the Roman Catholic Church—may soon confront Disciples with decisions which will have to be made about a common understanding of the church, including authority.

The following report is, therefore, a preliminary attempt of the Commission on Theology and Christian Unity to share "a word to the church" about the nature and expression of authority. We invite and hope for wider reflection and response by persons, congregations, ministerial groups, seminarians, and our ecumenical partners.

II. God's Authority

All genuine authority in the church is based upon and consonant with the nature of God as revealed in Jesus Christ. The Gospel—the proclamation of God's saving acts in the life, death, and resurrection of Jesus Christ—is the basis of all the church teaches and practices. It is the power of the crucified and risen Lord which is the "good news" which inspires and informs Christians as they seek to speak with authority in their witness.

It is important to realize that God's authority is significantly different from the understandings and exercise of authority in the secular world. There, as defined in *Webster's New World Dictionary,* authority is "the power or right to give commands, enforce obedience, take action, or make final decisions." This secular concept creeps into the church even through many traditional theological theories of authority which describe divine authority primarily in political metaphors and hierarchical patterns, e.g., King, Master, etc. History shows that this political definition assumes that power flows from those above (hierarchy) to those below, and thereby tends to encourage authoritarianism.

But to accept the crucified Christ as Lord requires a revision of certain understandings of God's ways and authority. The authority and power of God in Jesus Christ is, first, manifest in sacrificial *agape,* self-emptying servanthood, taking up the cause of the powerless, bearing the humiliating cross. "My power is made perfect in weakness" (2 Cor. 12:9) was God's reply to Paul's prayer for deliverance from suffering. Secondly, the authority of the crucified Christ is always a persuasive, not a coercive authority. Obedience is expressed in the covenant of love initiated in Jesus Christ. This authority is grounded, not in the exercise of force or manipulation, but in the divine promises of faithfulness, forgiveness, and salvation.

III. Authority in the Church

The church is a community called into being with vocation to proclaim and manifest the Gospel of God in Jesus Christ. Its very existence depends upon God's gracious election and God's abiding covenant of love. Its authority is evidenced when those in its fellowship find the means to be faithful to the will of their Lord. The quality of their inner life in the spirit brings a respect which allows them to speak in Christ's name with authority.

The church's authority comes as it accepts and fulfills three fundamental purposes:

(a) *Proclaiming the Good News* of God's act in Jesus Christ in word (teaching and preaching), in deed (mission and service), and in sacramental symbols (baptism and the Lord's Supper);

(b) *Acting in obedience* to God's commandment of love in self-sacrifice on behalf of

others and in a servant life in the world;

(c) *Caring for the upbuilding of the community* through worship and prayer, nurture and education, and mutual support and reconciling witness, and many forms of service within the community of believers and throughout the world, in order that the world may be given a credible, visible sign of God's reconciling love.

By virtue of this calling, the church always acknowledges that, in accord with the will of its Lord Jesus Christ, its authority is derivative. By this we mean that any authority claimed by the church is accepted in humility and gratitude for God's initiative. Those who speak and act for God are unworthy servants.

IV. God's Initiative and Our Response: The Character of Authority

The church accepts and exercises the authority it is given by God as a human response to divine initiative. The divine initiative in Jesus Christ creates genuine community, authentic selfhood, and true confidence in our response in faith. These are gifts of God which enable the church to test its own exercise of authority in the world. In *genuine community* the people of God are individually and corporately gathered by their common calling under the lordship of Christ, are renewed by the sacraments of baptism and the Lord's Supper, and are called to ministry. In expressing their *genuine selfhood* received in Christ, all Christians witness to the freedom and responsibility which expresses God's purposes for all humanity. In *genuine confidence* the gospel meets the deepest needs of the human condition, where the church works for the salvation of the world. The authority is an authority to empower love.

As authority is expressed by God, so it is responded to by God's people. One of the ways the church exercises this authority is through a process of corporate decision-making. Together, members of the Body of Christ attempt to witness to God's will. In this corporate process, however, each person in the faith community (Church) is aware of the fallibility of these attempts to communicate the Gospel. The fact that our response to God is fallible means we realize that the demands of the Gospel are greater than our ability to comprehend and express them perfectly. Decisions, therefore, are fallible, reformable, and ultimately subject to God's judgment. The church is repeatedly reminded that it is a fragile, earthen vessel.

V. Primary Witnesses to Christian Authority

The risen and living Christ is the ultimate authority for the Christian community. But two basic resources—Scripture and Tradition—have been provided to the church as authoritative witnesses to Jesus Christ and as guides in our task of spiritual discernment and guidance, Christian formation and ethics:

(a) *Scripture:* A unique and normative authority for the church is the Holy Scriptures, the written response to God's good news in Christ. Through their witness to God's saving action in the Old and New Testament made known in the history of Israel and the life of the earliest Christian communities, the church again and again receives its call to covenantal faithfulness. To those who accept its authority, this book becomes the Word God speaks to the church and the word God gives to the church to speak to the world.

(b) *Tradition:* There is an historic Christian Tradition to which all Christian bodies appeal in matters of faith and practice. By *Tradition* (with a capital "T") is meant the Gospel itself, transmitted from generation to generation in and by the whole life of the church as it is guided and nourished by the Holy Spirit, and as the Good News is expressed in teaching, worship and sacraments, witness, and ordered life.

Each generation of Christians is called upon to provide its own authentic, contemporary witness. The *Tradition* of the church is a resource for the proclamation, faithfulness, and upbuilding of the people of God. In addition to these two primary resources used in making judgments about God's will for us, the Christian Church (Disciples of Christ) also affirms the importance of reason and experience as authoritative in the life of Christians and the church to be used corporately and individually in discovering and interpreting God's will and mission.

VI. The Christian Church (Disciples of Christ): A Covenantal Community

Christians today live in an age of the divided church. We are assembled into communities of believers ordered by different polities and interpretations but who seek to manifest the one church of Jesus Christ. Each Christian community, including the Disciples of Christ, is called to reckon with the witness of the diverse and divided church in its worldwide expression, and to be receptive to the communication of the truth of the Gospel in other Christian communions. As the particular church it is, the Christian Church (Disciples of Christ) is called to render a faithful witness to the one Gospel which binds all followers of Christ together. Our history, our heritage, and our calling as a particular ordered community of faith is to promote the cause of unity among all Christians and to witness to the reconciliation of all of God's people.

The Christian Church (Disciples of Christ) has chosen for its life, relationships, and exercise of authority the model of covenant. This covenant extends the fellowship of this particular Christian communion to include and embrace the Church Universal. In obedience to God we seek to reach out to all who share a common faith, thereby strengthening our witness and broadening our vision beyond our limited perspectives. This is what the Christian Church (Disciples of Christ) means by "covenanting." We seek to live together in response to God's love within the body of Christ, the church. The continuing signs of our unity with other Christians in the one Gospel are baptism, communion, studying the Scriptures, sharing a common life.

At the heart of this covenant is God's love and call to free and responsible relationships in mutual trust. As a Christian community, the Christian Church (Disciples of Christ) accepts and exercises authority to undertake the global mission which God has granted to the church within covenantal bonds of freedom, responsibility, and accountability. For Disciples, authority is thus a *dispersed* and *shared* authority.

VII. Authority in the Ministry

In order to fulfill its mission, the church needs women and men who are publicly and continually *responsible* for pointing to its fundamental dependence on God as revealed in Jesus Christ. To those who are so called and ordained by the church, Christ bestows the gifts of ministry. Persons are called to the ordained ministry in differing ways. This call is discerned through personal prayer and reflection, through example, encouragement, and guidance coming from family, friends, congregations, and others. This call must be authenticated by the church's recognition of the gifts and graces of the particular person, both natural and spiritual.

Ordination is the action whereby some members of the Christian community are set apart for particular functions of ministry. Ordination is both act of God and act of the church. In ordaining, the Church, under the inspiration of the Holy Spirit, provides for the faithful proclamation of the Gospel and humble service in the name of Christ. The laying on of hands is the sign of the gift of the Spirit, rendering visible the fact that the ministry was instituted in the revelation accomplished in Christ, and reminding the church to look to him for the source of its commission. Properly speaking, then, ordination denotes an action of God and community by which the ordained are strengthened by the Spirit for their task and supported by the acknowledgment of the church.

Ordination is an action by and for the whole Christian community. Although ministers may serve local congregations, their ordination is to the ministry of the Church Universal. By receiving the minister in the act of ordination, the church acknowledges the minister's gifts and commits itself to recognize the validity of these gifts and be open to them. Likewise, the ordained offer their gifts to the church and commit themselves to the burden and opportunity of authority and responsibility. At the same time, they enter into a collegial relationship with other ordained ministers. Authority within the ordained ministry is personal, collegial, and communal.

Ordained ministers re-present to the church its own identity in Jesus Christ. As leaders and teachers they call the community to live under the authority of Christ, the teacher and prophet through whom law and prophecy were fulfilled. Their ministry should remind the community of God's eternal initiative towards God's people and of the dependence of the church on Jesus Christ, who is the source of its mission and the foundations of its unity.

The primary responsibility of ministers is to proclaim and witness to Jesus Christ, the Word of God. In this fundamental responsibility is the ground for their authority and responsibility. On the one hand, they are under divine obligation: "Necessity is laid upon me. Woe to me if I do not preach the Gospel!" On the other hand, they are under obligation to God's People—to Jew and Greek, slave and free, male and female. In fulfilling that obligation, they are ambassadors of Christ, bearers of the word of God, proclaimers of the Gospel which is the power of God. As witnesses to the divine word, the primary duties of the ministers are to preach and teach the Gospel, to celebrate the sacraments, to guide the life of the community in its worship, its mission and caring ministry.

In performing of these duties is the locus of ministerial authority. Ministerial authority is integral to the faithful proclamation of and witness to Jesus Christ. Compared with this central manifestation of God's power, all other concerns for authority are reduced in significance. When ministers are faithful in the witness to the Gospel, their ministerial authority will be recognized in other aspects of the church's life. However, since the authority of ministry is grounded in the authority of the servant who became obedient unto death, ministers must exercise authority in radical humility. Theirs is the authority of servanthood. In this lowly servanthood the power of God operates. The crucified Christ is the supreme manifestation of God's power; the power of Christ is made perfect in weakness.

Since the minister is ordained to the ministry of the whole church, ministerial leadership functions at every manifestation. At each place, the minister is responsible for preaching and teaching the word of God.

In the regional manifestation, leadership involves pastoral oversight (*episcope*), with particular responsibility for the congregations and ministers under its care. Regional ministers serve the church's continuity with the apostolic message. They foster the unity of the church's teaching, worship, and sacramental life. They have responsibility for leadership in the church's mission. They relate the Christian community in their region to the wider church, and the Church Universal to their congregations.

VIII. Authority in the Manifestations of the Church

In faith, Christians always seek to understand more fully the mystery of God which gives us life and salvation. We seek to pass on the Gospel and to participate in the world for the realization of God's Kingdom of peace and love. Our efforts at teaching Christ are impoverished and distorted, however, when we live the life of faith in a divided and partial community. Therefore, we deliberately bind ourselves to all who confess Jesus Christ as Lord and Savior. We try to listen to all who share our faith. This covenanting broadens our vision and strengthens our witness.

Because of the responsibility placed upon us as bearers of God's Gospel, we need to hear what others say, and to share with others what we believe. In this covenantal sharing of life, the church is empowered.

In fulfilling our call to witness to Christ, the Christian Church (Disciples of Christ) has ordered itself into three manifestations—congregational, regional, and general. Each of these is a manifestation of church. But the test for each lies in what sense it fosters wholeness, the embodiment of the unity for which Christ prayed. A local congregation cannot be truly faithful to Christ if it lives in isolation and does not foster wholeness. Likewise the region or the general church cannot make claims of sufficiency. Indeed, no manifestation of the Church can be Church without a covenant relation with the other two. Within these shared structures, all accept a shared authority and responsibility to witness to the Risen Lord together—in faith, ministry, and service. In this way each manifestation becomes an expression of the one Body of Christ.

IX. Conclusion

The Commission on Theology and Christian Unity believes that in seeking to understand these issues better, the Christian church (Disciples of Christ) will be able to fulfill our spiritual leadership, witness with authority, and respond to our calling to be part of the Body of Christ.

Commission on Theology and Christian Unity Members

William R. Baird
Walter D. Bingham
Eugene W. Brice
Paul A. Crow, Jr.
James O. Duke
Arla J. Elston
Wallace R. Ford
J. Jackson Forstman
Thomas Fountain
Howard Goodrich, Jr.
Robert K. Welsh *(staff)*
Ronald W. Graham
Kenneth E. Henry
Joe R. Jones
Vance Martin
Ronald E. Osborn
Albert M. Pennybacker
Narka Ryan
Robert A. Thomas
Ann Updegraff Spleth
Clark Williamson

Questions for Reflection and Discussion

1. The issue of authority and how this is defined in the context of Christian relationship undergirds the

discussion of polity. Unlike other secular groups, the church has people who are in authority and yet, they are not only in authority, they are in relationship as a part of the one body of Christ. We cannot be run as a typical business if we are to be faithful to the lifestyle of Christ. For him, the greatest were the least, and the least were the greatest. In light of this view, consider by what authority the church is called into relationship.

- By whose authority do we stay in relationship?
- By whose authority do we claim our mission and use our resources?
- As ones in relationship, how do we interpret the role of those who may disagree with specific actions of authority?
- By whose authority are their words heard?
- What specific issues of authority do you currently see as growing edges locally or at the regional or general levels?

2. For further study of the authority of scripture and norms for church life generally, see William Baird, *What Is Our Authority?*, listed in the bibliography as part of the Nature of the Church Series.

A Word to the Church on Ministry (1985)

I. The Ministry of God's People

As members of the Christian Church (Disciples of Christ) we acknowledge the life, death, and resurrection of Jesus Christ as a ministry of God to all humanity. Through the Holy Spirit, the whole people of God are called to share in Christ's ministry and are empowered to fulfill what that ministry requires. The special calling shared by all members of the church is to witness to the sovereign love of God, the grace of Jesus Christ, and the communion of the Holy Spirit in all of life. Through word and worship, service, and witness, we embody God's continuing work of creation and redemption.

As individuals and as a church we respond to the Word of God made known through the ministry of Jesus Christ. It is God's love that sustains and guides us as we exercise stewardship of God's bounty in our daily work, our use of natural resources, and our relations with all persons. We place the elements of our common life under the authority of Jesus Christ so that personally and as a church our living is changed and gives evidence of God's power at work within us.

Disciples of Christ have always believed that ministry belongs to the Church as a whole. All who are baptized are charged with the task of representing to the world, through every aspect of their lives, the will of God for all humanity. This conviction has found expression in our early opposition to viewing the ordained ministry as a class of Christians separate from the so-called "laity."

The ministry of God's people, the *laos* (the term that the New Testament in the original Greek uses for "people," which is the source of our English words "laity, laywomen, and laymen"), taken as a whole and in its diverse individual expressions, is to manifest and so continue the saving ministry of Jesus Christ. This ministry includes all members of the church joining together in witness to God's justice and reconciliation through worship together, daily work, sharing the Gospel, pastoral care, relief of human suffering, engagement in the struggle for peace and justice, and realization of the unity of the Church Universal. It is within this context of a shared ministry of the people of God that what is called "ordination" and "ordained ministry" is to be understood.

In claiming the ministry of the laos as the primary context for understanding the nature of ordained ministry, Disciples have borne a witness to the importance of the ministry of lay persons both within the church and the world. Several questions, however, need to be addressed more directly regarding the ministry of the laos as Disciples seek to articulate a more thorough theological understanding of ministry for the church in this generation:

1. How do we understand the relation of the ministry of God's people to the struggle for justice and liberation in our society and our world? What does it mean for us as Christians to offer the ministry of Christ in situations of conflict or controversy?

2. Should ministry be understood as daily work, whether it be as a homemaker, or teacher, or store clerk, or farmer? What then distinguishes the daily work of a Christian from that of a non-Christian?

3. If we identify ministry with every aspect of daily life and work, do we make the concept of ministry so broad as to lose any content or meaning?

4. How are God's people to understand our role as ministers/priests to one another and to non-believers? How do lay persons share the Gospel and care for the spiritual needs of individuals?

II. The Meaning of Ordination

In thinking of the Disciples of Christ, and in growing ecumenical understanding, all baptized believers are "ordained" to ministry. In baptism they become members of a royal priesthood, a holy nation, a people of God's own possession (1Peter 2:9). Thus it has been common to speak of the "priesthood of all believers"—the persons who live as faithful disciples of Jesus Christ in the church and in the world.

Traditionally it has also been common to speak of ordination, and of ordained ministries, with regard to a set-apart leadership. Ordination does not set one apart from the laos; rather, in recognizing God's call to particular individuals, the laos selects from its midst those persons to fulfill tasks and purposes necessary for the health, vitality, and effectiveness of the church's corporate ministry. By an act of ordination, which includes the ancient ceremony of the laying-on-of-hands and prayers for the Spirit, the church appoints persons to particular ministries. Ordination is thus a rite of the church in which the person ordained receives, by God's gracious action, a special calling to ministry.

Since the earliest era of the church's history, there has been a variety of patterns of ordained ministries, a rich and diverse terminology applied to these ministries, and many differing views with regard to their essential character. For this reason, it is important to seek to be as clear as possible about the theological bases for such ministries in the Christian Church (Disciples of Christ).

For Disciples the lay ministries and ordained ministries of the church are different forms of the one ministry of Jesus Christ that is shared by the entire People of God. Because they are forms of one ministry, they complement, support, and strengthen one another. It is with this understanding that Disciples speak of "ordination" and of an "ordering of ministry," so that lay and ordained ministries may be ordered in relation to one another for the upbuilding of the whole Christian community and life of the church.

By ordaining people to particular ministries, the church designates them to re-present to the church its own identity and calling in Jesus Christ. It is this re-presenting function, rather than amount of time (full-time or part-time) or kind of employment (salaried or non-salaried), that is the defining characteristic of the ordained ministries.

To say that ordained ministries are re-presentative does not mean that the ordained take on personal or official status superior to that of the non-ordained. There are no differences of status or worth between lay persons and ordained persons, for in their diversity these different ministries are mutually dependent, mutually complementary, and mutually enriching. Neither does it mean that they undertake ministries so that those who are not ordained may be relieved of their own ministerial responsibilities. Rather, they are ordained to re-present (i.e., to present again, to show forth) to the whole people the ministry it has received in Christ Jesus. In this way those ordained carry a special ministry, which is not different in kind, but distinctive in its focus in equipping, nurturing, guiding, and setting before the church the ministry shared by all.

Ordination sets one apart for leadership in the life and witness of the church. While the ordained ministry cannot be reduced to any mere listing of tasks, it may be identified by leadership with regard to three fundamental aspects of the church's life and witness:

1. acting in obedience to God's commandment of love in self-sacrifice on behalf of others and in a servant life in the world;
2. proclaiming the gospel by word (teaching and preaching), by sacramental actions (Baptism and the Lord's Supper), and by deed (mission and service);
3. overseeing the life of the community in its worship, education, witness, mission, fellowship, and pastoral nurture.

In selecting men and women for ordination, the church thus seeks to insure that its ministry of service, proclamation, and oversight shall be constantly held up before its members and furthered by good order.

In ordination the church gives grateful acknowledgment to God who in every age grants to women and men the spiritual gifts necessary for such ministry. In making decisions about whom to ordain, the church looks to the personal, inward call from God, which leads persons to seek such ministry, to the God-given gifts, to the personal characteristics and aptitudes, and to the background and promise (e.g., education, skills, etc.) that candidates have for effective ministry. On these judgments the church issues its approval, appointment, and ordination.

In light of this understanding of ordination, the Commission on Theology believes that Disciples might well consider the following questions:

1. Should Disciples ordain persons apart from a call to a particular representative assignment? Is there value in our present practice of ordaining and setting persons apart for leadership in the church prior to their receiving a call to service from a particular expression of the church's life (congregation, educational institution, regional ministry, etc.)? Are there dangers in this practice?

2. Who should be responsible for the service of ordination by which the church sets apart its leaders? Can there be any justification for assigning this task to the person being ordained since ordination is the action of Christ through the Church? Should this not be the responsibility of the church and its regional commissions on the ministry?

3. How can Disciples make greater use of the gifts for representing the church's identity and calling in Jesus Christ that God gives to women and ethnic minorities?

III. A Proposal for Discussion: One Order—Three Offices

The history of the church has been marked by several different patterns, or orderings, of ordained ministries. The exclusive warrant of the New Testament Scriptures cannot be claimed for any one. Each were forms adapted to the needs of the churches in different times and places. And no single pattern was set down by Jesus or the authors of the New Testament as *the* model of the church's ministry or its authority.

Growing out of its discussion regarding the meaning and practice of ministry within the Christian Church (Disciples of Christ) as we look to the future, the Commission on Theology commends for consideration a *single order of ordained ministry which would include three offices.* This pattern appears to be in line with the emerging consensus within the ecumenical movement and is the current pattern accepted by many churches throughout the world, e.g., Anglican, Methodist, Roman Catholic, Orthodox, Lutheran, and United Churches. It thus appears to offer a strong possibility for wider ecumenical relationships in the future. This pattern of ministerial leadership corresponds to the three aspects of the church's life identified by the Commission as fundamental (refer to Section II, paragraph 7): (a) the ministry of service to church and world (the *diaconate*, or deacons); (b) the ministry of proclamation by Word and Sacrament (the *presbyterate*, or pastors or ministers); and, (c) the ministry of oversight (the *episcopate*, or bishops).

The threefold order of ministry proposed for consideration is not three different orders of ministry with three different ordinations, but one order of ministry with one ordination. The three offices proposed would supersede the current office of the ordained minister now identified in *The Design of the Christian Church (Disciples of Christ)* in recognition of the different tasks fulfilled by those ordained to ministry in the church. Although Disciples do not commonly use the terms "deacon," "presbyter," and "bishop" when referring to their ordained ministers, and would probably not do so in the future, the fundamental tasks associated with each of these offices are currently performed by ordained ministers. For example, Disciples have deacons—that is, persons who give leadership to the ministry of service to church and world—but we call them "Administrator of the Week of Compassion," or "Executive Director of a Christian Home," or "Fraternal Worker in Zaire." Disciples also have presbyters—persons who give leadership to the ministry of proclamation by Word and Sacrament—but we call them "Minister," or "Minister of Education," or "Pastor." Similarly, Disciples have bishops—persons who give leadership to the ministry of oversight—but we call them "Regional Minister," or "Area Minister," or "General Minister and President."

Several issues speak to this proposal for a threefold order of ordained ministry. First, there is some biblical precedent for such offices in the life of the church (Acts 6:1–6; 15:13–22; 13:1; 1 Cor. 12:28; Phil. 1:1). Second, in the history of the church this pattern has emerged as predominant, but in different forms, for example, among Episcopalians, Roman Catholics, Orthodox, Methodists, and Lutherans. Third, in the theological discussion of the World Council of Churches and within the Consultation on Church Union, this pattern has been offered as an invitation to all churches to move toward the full mutual reconciliation of ministries. Fourth, and perhaps most significant theologically, it embraces the various types of representative functions essential to the identity and calling of the church in its service, proclamation, mission, and unity.

In each of the offices of the threefold ordained ministry being proposed, one aspect of the church's life and witness comes into particular focus:

- In the ministry of the *deacon*, the active witness and mission of the church as servant is assisted and advanced.
- In the ministry of the *presbyter*, the proclamation, preaching, teaching, and sacramental dimensions (presiding at the Table and administering Baptism) of the church are lifted up.
- In the ministry of the *bishop*, the oversight of the life of the community comes into focus.

Thus, within a single order of ordained ministry, there can be three distinct offices that are at the same time mutually supportive and interrelated. The threefold ordained ministry, taken as a whole, thus re-presents the fundamental characteristics of ministry shared by all baptized believers.

Licensed Ministers

The threefold order of ordained ministry being proposed for consideration does not include "the licensed minister" as an office. The Commission believes that licensed ministry would need to be continued as part of the total ministry of the Christian Church (Disciples of Christ); however, greater clarity needs to be given to the relationship between licensed ministry and ordained ministry—that is, licensed ministers would be persons *preparing* for ordination, or *serving* as ministers in special circumstances. The value of this arrangement is the identification of the *order* of ministry with the act of *ordination*. Although *The Design* currently identifies licensed ministers as an "office" in a two-fold order of ministry, the understanding of licensed minister being recommended here for consideration is consistent with the Disciples tradition, which has always distinguished "licensed ministry" from "ordained ministry."

Congregational Offices: Elder and Deacon

The recommendation of a threefold order of ministry that would replace the current office of the ordained minister leaves unaddressed the congregational offices of elder and deacon. There is a great deal of diversity in our present practice and understanding of these offices, especially the office of elder. For some of our congregations, elders are ordained and carry responsibility for leadership at the Lord's Supper. For other congregations, elders are elected and installed—but not ordained—and carry similar functions of ministry at the Table.

This issue is not simply one of consistency or order; indeed, Disciples cherish their freedom to have a rich diversity in practice in such matters (and as a Commission, we want to underscore our support for such diversity in the life of the church). However, in ecumenical discussions it is difficult to know how to describe our eldership in such a way as to be claimed by other churches as part of the larger theological understanding of the church's ministry.

We believe that the congregational offices of elder and deacon (i.e., non-professional, non full-time) have a valid place within the total ministry of the Church Universal. The Commission believes these offices represent a valuable contribution by Disciples to the emerging theological consensus within the ecumenical movement as they bear witness to the essential ministry of lay persons. We want to celebrate the participation of such offices within the sacramental ministry of the church.

Issues for Discussion

We believe this proposal for one order of ordained ministry with three offices raises the following questions which have not been addressed:

1. How do you respond to the proposal of a single order of ordained ministry with three offices? Could such a threefold order enable Disciples to grow in our understanding of the calling of the church to ministries of service, proclamation, and pastoral oversight?

2. Do you believe we could have a threefold order which would continue to use a variety of titles for those holding different positions in ministry?

3. How fluid are the three offices within a single order of ministry? In other words, would one move from *presbyter* to *bishop*, and back again in the course of one's ministry? Or is such a move (from *presbyter* to *bishop*) seen to be "for life"?

4. Given the identification of licensed ministry as a category in relation to ordained ministry, what responsibility do our regional Commissions on Ministry have for the nurture and care of licensed ministers, both persons preparing for ordination and persons serving as ministers in special circumstances?

5. Are congregational elders and deacons to be ordained? If so, should they be ordained for life, or for a set term?

6. How can greater collegiality be expressed between the ordained pastor and the eldership within a congregation in order to assure that these ministries are not seen to be over against one another?

7. How may we expand our current understanding and practice of the eldership and diaconate to include a ministry of teaching, shepherding, and governance beyond the limited role of most Disciples elders and deacons as those who "pray or serve at the Table"?

IV. The Ministry of Oversight

As the Commission discussed this proposal of "one order–three offices," the focus of our work centered upon only one of the three offices: the ministry of oversight (*episcope*). It is here that Disciples have often had the most difficulty, for our history has often been marked by a rejection of any authority for church life beyond the congregation, as well as a fear of abuses of power and authority which have taken place in other denominations or communions which have a recognized ministry of *episcope*. This document does not, therefore, set forth detailed descriptions of the ministry of service (deacons) or the ministry of Word and Sacrament (presbyters). Those will be dealt with in detail in the future work of the Commission.

A. The Meaning of Oversight for Disciples

Oversight (*episcope*) has been an aspect of ministry since the beginning of the New Testament church. After Philip had preached the Gospel in Samaria, the leaders of the Jerusalem Church sent Peter and John to confirm the mission and pray for the converts (Acts 8:14). When Paul and Barnabas visited the churches that they had founded in Asia Minor, they appointed elders (*presbyters*) in each congregation (Acts 14:23). According to Acts 20:28, Paul exhorted the elders of the Ephesian Church to guard the flock for which the Holy Spirit had made them overseers. Paul admonished members of the churches he had founded to respect their leaders who were "over them in the Lord" and who were responsible for their admonition and instruction (cf. 1 Cor. 16:16; 1 Thess. 5:12). In addressing the church at Philippi, Paul gave special attention to the bishops (*episkopoi*) and the deacons (*diakonoi*) (Phil. 1:1). Titus is instructed by Paul to appoint elders (*presbyteroi*) or bishops (*episkopoi*) in every city of Crete (Titus 1:5–7). These leaders were to be chosen according to well-defined standards, and were qualified to be overseers of the church's life and teachers of the apostolic faith.

As the church moved into the second century, and the distance from the event of God's disclosure in Jesus Christ and the normative witness to that event in the proclamation of the apostles became greater, there arose a need for a more deliberate ordering of the church's life to insure faithfulness in the observance of Baptism and the Lord's Supper, and for maintaining the continuity with the apostolic message. To this end, the ministry of oversight (*episcope*) became more formalized in the life of the church.

The shape of that ministry was well defined by the two terms which Paul had used for the Philippian leaders:

episkopos and *diakonos*. The former was borrowed from the Greco-Roman economy where it represented over-sight as exercised, for example, by the steward of an estate. The latter was used in New Testament times for an ordinary household servant: a waiter on tables. Thus, the ministry of oversight in the early church was characterized by a type of supervision that was designed to serve.

Although early Disciples leaders were rightly opposed to a clericalism, which dominated the church, at the same time they recognized the importance of the ministry of oversight or *episcope*. This recognition rested on their acknowledgment of the authority of the biblical witness and their conviction that all things should be done decently and in order. For example, Alexander Campbell did not hesitate to use the term "bishop," and by it he stressed the responsibility of the "bishops" (in Greek, *episkopoi*) or "elders" of the congregation for shepherding and teaching the members and for leading in worship and in ministering Baptism and the Lord's Supper.

As early as the 1850s, Disciples had state evangelists (later called state secretaries or executive secretaries) who exercised some oversight in the life of the congregations by offering instruction in local church management and the practical meaning of the Christian faith. In 1886, Black Disciples in North Carolina met in assembly to set standards for their pastors and to authorize recommended standards and procedure for ordination as part of their responsibility for overseeing the general life of their congregations. In the 1930s, as a legitimate function of the total church in assembly, International Conventions began to recommend to all Disciples congregations standards and procedures for ordination, for the church's well-being.

In the 1960s ordination was recognized to be the responsibility of the whole church with established state (regional) or area committees as the locus for supervising all ordinations. Executive Secretaries of the state organizations (later to be called Regional Ministers) played a major role in the location and relocation of ministers. They also functioned in various informal ways to provide leadership and supervision to congregations in their states.

We have seen in Scripture, in the early church, and in our history as Disciples of Christ, that the ministry of oversight (*episcope*) is an important dimension of the re-presentative character of all forms of ministry: pastors, elders, deacons; congregational and regional boards; the General Assembly and General Board of the Christian Church (Disciples of Christ); regional and general unit staff; etc. We are also aware that this ministry is already being exercised among us: members of congregations *oversee* programs in Christian education, in evangelism, in administration and stewardship, Christian witness and mission, and in worship and the fellowship life of the total congregation. Many congregations have also developed "shepherding programs" so that the ministry of oversight is one extended to, as well as exercised by, all members of the church.

The ministry of *episcope* is thus shared by the whole people of God, the laos. At times, however, it comes to greater focus and expression in some forms of ministry than in others. For the Christian Church (Disciples of Christ) with our strong emphasis upon the congregation as a primary place for the experience of church, the focus for oversight is most often centered around the ministry of pastors, elders, and deacons. Just as there is the need for a focus of ministry in particular persons within a congregation, there is a similar need for such a focus in persons responsible for the care, nurture, growth, and teaching of congregations within a region, as well as the need for a ministry of pastor-to-pastors. One may also identify the ministry of oversight in relation to the general manifestation of church in its tasks and services to congregations and regions and the wider programs of overseas ministries, higher education, benevolent work, ecumenical involvements, and Christian education. However, for our discussion at this time in our history, primary attention to the exercise of the ministry of *episcope* needs to be focused upon understanding the ministry of oversight in its regional manifestation.

B. *The Ministry of* Episcope *and the Region as Church*

Perhaps one of the clearest areas where the ministry of oversight (*episcope*) finds expression within the Christian Church (Disciples of Christ) as we have developed through the restructure process is that of the regional manifestation of church. It is in the regional minister where elements of the episcopal ministry are currently lodged, and yet, at the same time, where that ministry needs to be more clearly defined and understood.

The Commission has identified six elements that we believe should mark the ministry of true *episcope* throughout the whole ministry of the church, but particularly in relation to the regional minister. These elements would enable and guide oversight throughout the church in all its manifestations in the church's efforts to be a faithful and continuing witness to the apostolic word and worship—where the Word is preached and the sacraments observed.

1. Those who are appointed to the specific ministry of *episcope* within a region are charged to serve as personal representatives of the given unity of the church in all places and all ages. Regional ministers should seek to make visible to the church its unity, and to call it to greater unity within and among the congregations in a region, as well as the reconciliation of all the churches and communions globally with one another.

2. Regional ministers have the task, individually and collegially, to proclaim, teach, and pass on the apostolic Christian faith as it is witnessed to in Scripture and Tradition, thus assuring continuity of witness from generation to generation. They also bear the responsibility of helping the church to understand the changing situations it faces in its own life and in the world, and to interpret the Christian faith appropriately and intelligibly in ever-new situations. They will understand themselves as teachers of the faith in the region.

3. One task of the episcopal office is that of general pastoral oversight of all members of the church in a given region. This entails a regular and frequent presence in each congregation for the purposes of preaching, teaching,

celebrating of the Lord's Supper, and participating in services of Baptism and ordination. In this context, the regional minister has a direct responsibility to be a pastor to the pastors in the region.

4. Regional ministers should bear responsibility for leadership in the church's mission to the world. Theirs is the task of voicing and articulating the command of God that justice be done. More than ever before, Christians are now aware of the unity of the whole world—we sink or swim together.

5. The organized life and work of the church in a region also requires oversight. However, the regional minister is not just a programmatic functionary comparable to the secular executive who sees to it that the job gets done. As a teacher of the Christian faith, the regional minister bears special responsibility to reflect theologically upon this work, and by delegation to and cooperation with other members of the church, to see that it is done properly.

6. Working collegially with congregations and members of the church, the regional minister has a particular responsibility to oversee the ordination of candidates for the order of ministry. Regional ministers should either be present or represented at services of ordination. It is also their responsibility to exercise care and oversight for all candidates to the ordained ministry through regional commissions on ministry.

One of the carry-overs from our historic concerns about "clericalism" in the church and the abuse of the power and authority of bishops as seen in other denominations has been a strong reluctance among Disciples to use the term "bishop" or to see the ministry of oversight (*episcope*) as part of the wider ministry of the church. And yet, we are also aware that in the establishment of regional offices, we have in fact developed an *episcope* which may be functioning without a clear theological or constitutional foundation. Any understanding and practice of *episcope* among Disciples must be developed in terms of its ministerial and pastoral functions, and not in relation to magisterial or hierarchical exercise of authority. In the best of situations regional ministers function collegially and exercise authority as that of a "shepherd" or "pastor to pastors."

There is a need, therefore, to understand the practice of *episcope* within the Disciples as we develop a fuller statement on ministry and the Church. The following questions are set forth as beginning points for such consideration:

1. Are we able to see the "ministry of oversight" as set forth earlier in this report as a primary function of the total ministry of the church which is exercised by several offices of ordained ministers in the different manifestations of our church—sometimes as a local pastor; sometimes as a regional minister; sometimes as a general unit executive?

2. Can we pursue this discussion about *episcope* in some fresh ways which would bring our Disciples strong commitment to collegiality in ministry to be a part of the wider ecumenical discussions of the office of bishop?

3. In the light of Scripture, Tradition, and our own history, are we as a church, ready to own and name the ministry of *episcope* that is already being exercised by and among us? Should we begin using the title "bishop"? Or, could we identify the functions and the tasks of the episcopal ministry, and then worry about the title?

4. How would the structure of our present regional ministries need to change in order for regional ministers more fully to exercise the ministry of pastoral oversight? Are our regions too large for effective pastor oversight to congregations and pastors by the regional minister?

5. If regional ministers are to exercise *episcope* collegially with one another (as well as with the whole church), would the Council of Ministers occupy a more important place in our polity?

6. Do those who are ministers in the general manifestation of church also bear a responsibility for the ministry of *episcope*? Do they not show forth the unity of the church, teach and pass on the apostolic faith, serve as pastors to the whole church, and lead it in mission to the world?

7. In which office of ordained ministry would campus ministers, chaplains, and full-time staff to ecumenical organizations and agencies be located? Are these diaconal ministers of service? Or ministers of oversight?

Members of the Commission on Theology

William R. Baird	Walter D. Bingham
Paul A. Crow, Jr.	James O. Duke
Arla J. Elston	Wallace R. Ford
Thomas Fountain	H. Jackson Forstman, *Chair*
Beverly R. Gaventa	Howard B. Goodrich, Jr.
Ronald W. Graham	Kenneth E. Henry
Joe R. Jones	Michael Kinnamon
Vance Martin	Ronald E. Osborn
A. M. Pennybacker	Narka Ryan
Ann Updegraff Spleth	Robert K. Welsh *(Staff)*
Clark K. Williamson	

Questions for Reflection and Discussion

1. Discuss the questions listed in "The Ministry of God's People" (p. 95) and "The Meaning of Ordination" (p. 98).
2. Discuss how to present the "Issues for Discussion" (pp. 101–102) to your local faith community. What would the community need in order to facilitate a productive discussion about these issues and avoid a mere pooling of opinions, which may or may not be well-informed or reasoned?
3. Discuss the questions listed in "The Ministry of *Episcope* and the Region as Church" (p. 108). Consider inviting an area or regional staff person to participate in this discussion, or visit your area or regional office to learn more about their work.
4. For further study on the topic of ministry, refer to *Ministry Among Disciples: Past, Present, and Future* by D. Newell Williams, listed in the bibliography as part of the Nature of the Church Series.
5. Invite an area or regional minister to join the group as you consider the various forms of ordaining, licensing, commissioning, and installing individuals among Disciples and in churches of various denominations. What is the purpose of ordaining? How is this practice understood in a variety of ways? What is the purpose of licensing, commissioning, or installing?

A Word to the Church on Baptism (1987)

I. Baptism in the New Testament

As Disciples of Christ we have always sought to derive our interpretations of the meaning and practice of Christian baptism from the understandings of the early church as reflected in the New Testament. This has led some Disciples to think that the New Testament clearly discloses the baptismal practice of the early church and that in the New Testament interpretations of the meaning of baptism were relatively unimportant. Study of the New Testament, however, requires a more careful reading of the texts regarding baptism. On the one hand, New Testament texts on baptism offer a rich diversity in their interpretations of its meaning. On the other hand, the New Testament contains very little information about how early Christians actually practiced baptism. After all, the writers of the New Testament had no need to describe their practice since their communities would have known how baptism was carried out in various locales. By contrast, explaining the meaning and significance of Christian baptism was crucial, for ritual washings were common in Judaism as well as in other Greco-Roman religions, making it essential to distinguish the baptism of Christians.

Early Christian *interpretations* of baptism often trace Christian baptism to the life of Jesus. We find within the New Testament two important claims about the baptism of Jesus. First, the Gospel writers include Jesus among those baptized in the renewal movement led by John the Baptist. The Gospel writers testify to Jesus' baptism, and they locate in that event divine approval of Jesus and the beginning of his ministry (Mark 1:9–11, Matthew 3:13–17, Luke 3:21–22, John 1:29–34).

Along with this baptism by John, Gospel tradition also identifies Jesus' death as a form of baptism. In Mark and Luke, Jesus anticipates his death and refers to it as "the baptism with which I am baptized" (Mark 10:38–40, Luke 12:50). Some scholars also see in John's Gospel an allusion to the baptism of Jesus' death when, at his crucifixion, both blood and water flow from his pierced side (John 19:34).

The early Christian interpretation of baptism best known to Disciples connects itself with Jesus' baptism by John. John's baptism for forgiveness is recalled in Acts, when Peter's Pentecost sermon urges baptism: "Repent, and be baptized every one of you in the name of Jesus Christ for the forgiveness of your sins; and you shall receive the gift of the Holy Spirit. For the promise is to you and to your children and to all that are far off, every one whom the Lord our God calls to him." (Acts 2:38–39). Throughout Acts, baptism follows repentance in response to the preaching of the Gospel (Acts 8:12, 9:18, etc.; cf. 1Peter 3:21). While the leaders of the church administer baptism, Acts makes it clear that baptism stems from the grace of God (see, for example, Acts 10:44–48, where the gift of the Holy Spirit falls on Cornelius and his household, persuading Peter that he must not withhold baptism).

By contrast with Acts, which primarily sees baptism as bringing about the forgiveness of sins, Paul interprets baptism as incorporation. He identifies the baptism of believers with that of Jesus at his crucifixion: "Do you not know that all of us who have been baptized into Christ Jesus were baptized into his death? We were buried therefore with him by baptism into death, so that as Christ was raised from the dead by the glory of the Father, we too might walk in newness of life" (Romans 6:3–4). For Paul, the gift of baptism confers on the individual both a new identity and a new community. The baptized, by being baptized into Christ or into the name of Christ (1 Corinthians 1:13, Galatians 3:27), receive a new identity.

Paul's frequent references to baptism in Christ have almost spatial connotation. Believers are moved from one sphere (the old age, the power of sin) to another sphere in which God's reign is being made manifest. It is for this reason that Paul can speak of being purchased by God(1 Corinthians 7:23) or being seized by Christ (Philippians 3:12). Believers belong to Christ in his death and receive the promise that they also will belong to Christ when his power is revealed to all of creation (1 Corinthians 15:20—28). The second-century Christian leader Ignatius captured this sense of belonging well when he wrote that Christians are "stamped with the Father's name" (cf. Matthew 28:19).

While baptism involves the individual, baptism does not leave the individual isolated but firmly placed within a new community. It is not accidental that Paul refers to baptism when he addresses believers at Corinth about their quarrels and dissensions (1 Corinthians 1:10–17, 12:13). Believers constitute one body *because* they are baptized *into* one body. It is on this basis that Paul can and does attack the notion that individual gifts or individual behaviors influence only the life of the individual.

In these early generations, then, baptism was not merely a rite of initiation. On the contrary, it marked a radical break in the life of the believer. New Testament writers recognize that growth and maturity occur after baptism, but they nevertheless see baptism as incorporation into Christ which has profound implications for the individual (Galatians 3:27–28).

These texts and others challenge Disciples to recover the *significance* of baptism, but they offer little assistance to us as we consider our *practice* of baptism. While it is true that the narratives of Acts name only adults who are baptized, it is also important to recall that in Acts 2:39, Peter announces God's promise "to you and to your children." In addition, Acts refers to the baptism of entire households (Acts 10:23–48, 16:25–34), a baptism which may have included infants, since all those dependent on the head of a house were regarded as part of a household; 1 Corinthians 7:14, which refers to the sanctification of children by their parents' faith may indicate that infants were baptized.

Difficulties also arise concerning the method of baptism. The Greek verb *baptizein* (to baptize) has connotations of washing or immersion, but it is impossible to conclude from this use of the word what actual early Christian practice may have been. The difficulties involved in reconstructing early Christian practice become clear when we acknowledge the variety of practices referred to in the New Testament itself. Some Christians receive the gift of the Holy Spirit prior to baptism (Acts 10:44–48, 11:15–18), while others receive the Spirit only after baptism (Acts 8:14–17). Some who are called disciples apparently still practice the baptism of John (Acts 19:1–7). According to Paul, some even practice baptism on behalf of the dead (1 Corinthians 15:29). Our earliest evidence of actual practice may come from the *Didache*, an early Christian manual of instruction, which states that running water should be used if available but, in the absence of running water, water should be poured on the head of the baptismal candidate. While the *Didache* is not scriptural, it does indicate that at least for one early Christian community, immersion is the preferred but not the only form of baptism.

As in our considerations of other elements of Christian faith and practice, it is important to ask what sort of guidance the Bible provides for us regarding baptism (See "A Word to the Church on Authority"). Writers of the biblical texts proclaimed God's word as a challenge to their generations, and we are likewise obliged not merely to repeat those formulations, but to ask how God's word addresses us. On the issue of baptism, it is clear that the New Testament is far more interested in what baptism signifies about new life than in the age of the candidate or the manner of baptism. While Paul speaks of the importance of baptism, he clearly subordinates it to the proclamation of the gospel. Indeed, baptism is only important as it is a proclamation of the gospel (1 Cor. 1:17). It is essential for Disciples to learn from this priority if we are to reclaim and hand on the meaning of baptism in this generation.

II. The Disciples' Baptismal Heritage

Alexander Campbell and those associated with him in the beginnings of the Disciples' movement understood themselves as continuing the work begun by Martin Luther and the Protestant Reformation of the 16th century. Indeed, Campbell's followers called themselves "reformers." Nowhere is this self-understanding of the early Disciples clearer than in their views of the theology and practice of baptism. Accordingly this overview of the Disciples tradition with regard to baptism begins with the Reformation.

Luther regarded baptism (along with the Lord's Supper) as a sacrament because in it there are combined two things: the promise of God's gracious forgiveness of our sins and a concrete sign (water and the action of baptizing). The chief point about baptism, for Luther, is the grace of God: "the divine promise, which says: 'He that believeth and is baptized shall be saved' (Mark 16:16)." Baptism is not a "good work" and justifies no one; "rather, faith in the word of the promise to which baptism was conjoined, is what justifies, and so completes, that which the baptism signified." The point of baptism, what Campbell would later call the "design" of it, has everything to do with God's grace and faith as the appropriate response to it.

Secondly, Luther held that because baptism symbolizes death and resurrection as the fulfilling and completion of justification, immersion is the form which gives "the sign of baptism as fully and completely as possible." However, according to Luther, immersion is not necessary (although it is preferable), that is, it is not the only legitimate form of baptism. He argued that to withhold baptism from children would imply that the good news depends on our ability to receive it, which would be "works-righteousness" all over again. He held to his position because of his emphasis that justification is by grace through faith and because infant baptism well reflects our dependence on God's grace. The later Disciples will agree with Luther that the form—what Campbell called the "mode" of baptism—should be immersion, but would stress the importance of the response of faith in such a way as to exclude infant baptism. In this, they understood themselves to be carrying the insights of the Reformation through to a more consistent practice.

Campbell's most thorough discussion of baptism occurs in *The Christian System,* in a chapter that opens with this remark: "Luther said that the doctrine of justification, or forgiveness, was the test of a standing or falling church...We agree with him in this...." In *The Millennial Harbinger* of 1847 he called baptism "a sort of embodiment of the gospel." Of it, he remarked: "We do not place baptism amongst good works....In baptism we are passive in everything but in giving our consent." This discussion of grace, justification, and forgiveness is all part of what Campbell called the "meaning" or "design," the "end" (purpose) of baptism. It is clear throughout his writings on baptism, from his often repeated declarations, that the design of baptism—justification by grace—is by far the most important point to be understood.

Campbell also stressed two other points about baptism. They were that the proper *subject* for baptism is a penitent believer—not an infant or child and not merely an adult, but a *believer*—and that the proper, indeed the only proper, mode of baptism is immersion in water, in the name of the Father, Son, and Holy Spirit.

Campbell held to these views for a set of clearly stated reasons. First, the New Testament appeared to Campbell to be silent on any form of baptism other than that of baptizing believing adults. Second, the meaning of the word *baptizein*, so Campbell contended, seemed perfectly clear: immersion is the only possible way to interpret it. Third, he was trying to reform the church and he saw the combination between the state-church and infant baptism as nothing less than disastrous. The uncritical absorption of a whole populace into the church results in the loss of any distinction between the church and the world. Referring to a period in Scottish history when the whole nation was baptized, he states that "all the enormities [great evils] committed in the realm were committed by members of the church." If the church is to be a "a peculiar people," Campbell concluded, infant baptism indiscriminately practiced must be replaced with baptism of penitent believers.

Stone's views of baptism were much the same as Campbell's. In his autobiography he tells how he came to the view that "baptism was ordained for the remission of sins, and ought to be administered in the name of Jesus to all believing penitents." As had Campbell, Stone grounded his views on the Reformation principles *sola gratia, sola fide* (by grace alone, by faith alone). "No good works," says Stone, "no qualifications are previously required"—not even the emotionally wrenching experiences of people in frontier revivals.

Stone was also similar to Campbell in holding the view that baptism should not be administered indiscriminately. He maintained that "the church must exercise care to determine whether applicants for baptism are true penitents if it is to remain a church." And Stone also thought that immersion is the proper form (mode) of baptism, although he refused to make this question a test of fellowship and communion.

The subsequent discussion of baptism among Disciples has tended to suffer from a lack of adequate understanding of Campbell and Stone. The era from Campbell's death in 1866 to the early 20th century saw the hardening of their views into a new dogma. This period, referred to as the time of Disciples' scholasticism, compares to the generation of the founders as 17th-century Protestant scholasticism compares to the 16th-century reformers. Dynamic encounter with grace became calcified into formulas. This epoch of Disciples development corresponded to the rise of fundamentalism in America and was influenced by it.

In the era of Disciples scholasticism, the only baptismal issue was that of the mode of baptism—immersion. Although Campbell was more insistent upon immersion than was Stone, nonetheless he subordinated it in importance to the meaning of baptism (the remission of sins), to the subject of baptism (penitent believers), and to the ecclesial character of baptism (in baptism the church constitutes itself and therefore baptism should not be indiscriminately practiced). As the movement became legalistic, all this tended to be forgotten for the sake of an exclusive emphasis on immersion. Consequently much of the reaction of liberal Disciples to Disciples fundamentalism was similarly distorted.

The task for Disciples today is the critical reappropriation of the fullness of their tradition in the context of the wider ecumenical discussion with a willingness to learn from others and a modest confidence that the Disciples tradition itself, at its best, is a distinctive theological contribution to the larger church.

Particularly we should reappropriate the following from our tradition: (1) a witness to the importance of believers' baptism as yes-saying to God's grace, (2) a concern with the life of both individual Christians and the church as pointing to the way of life that the church is to represent to the world, and (3) a commitment to baptism as the sacrament of unity, and (4) the priority of God's grace. We should also be aware of the social and historical relativity of our tradition and should particularly seek to avoid all "works-righteousness"; that is, we may not make believers' baptism a condition of receiving God's grace, apart from which God is not free to be a gracious God. This would go entirely against the grain of the Disciples' heritage.

III. The Nature of Baptism

Baptism is a public act by which the church proclaims God's grace, as revealed in the life, death, and resurrection of Jesus Christ, through the use of a visible sign of God's gracious initiative and the human individual's response in faith. With other Christians we affirm that as baptism is at once divine gift and human response, it marks the beginning of the Christian life and looks toward lifelong growth into the fullness of faith.

Baptism, as a gift of grace, received by faith, expresses its meaning in a variety of images. Baptism is new birth (John 3:5); it is God's gift of life—a radical new beginning. Baptism is a washing with water(1 Corinthians 6:11); it is a cleansing from sin—a sign of God's forgiving grace. Baptism is putting on clothing (Galatians 3:27); it is to put on Christ—it is to receive a new identity. Baptism is death and resurrection in unity with Christ (Romans 6:3–11); it is the crucifixion of the old, separate self, and the resurrection to new life in the body of Christ. Baptism conveys the gift of the Spirit (Acts 2:38); it is the power of new life now and the pledge of life in the age to come (2 Corinthians 1:22). In marking a new identity with Christ, baptism is a mandate for discipleship as part of the Christian community in service to the world. Thus, the meaning of baptism is grounded in God's redemptive action in Christ, it incorporates the believer in the community in the body of Christ, and it anticipates life in the coming age when the powers of the old world will be overcome, and the purposes of God will triumph (1 Corinthians 15:28).

Traditionally, Disciples have preferred to call baptism an ordinance rather than a sacrament. The term "sacrament" seemed to represent a kind of sacramentalism which understood the sacraments as the exclusive channels of God's grace, and the special prerogative of a sacerdotal hierarchy. However, Disciples have increasingly come to recognize that the term "ordinance" is subject to misunderstanding whereby the ordinances are taken as orders to be legalistically obeyed, and thus transformed into human works rather than signs of God's grace. A proper understanding indicates that a sacrament is an expression of God's grace in a visible sign. In the case of baptism, the sign is an act of using water—a common element, essential for life. Therefore, baptism can be appropriately called a sacrament or an ordinance of the church. It may be called a sacrament of the church because in this sign the grace of God is made focally present. It may be called an ordinance of the church because as God's gift by which persons are formally incorporated into the body of Christ, it is one means by which the church orders its life and distinguishes itself from the world.

Most churches involved in the ecumenical movement acknowledge the two essential elements—divine grace and human response—constitutive of the meaning of baptism. Their baptismal practices, however, represent differing views of the way the act may properly be said to relate grace and faith.

Churches that practice "infant baptism" stress the gracious initiative of God, while also affirming that a response of faith is made by the parents and community at the time of baptism and by the individual at a later moment through confirmation. Churches that practice "believers' baptism" stress the significance of the individual decision of faith at the time of baptism, while also affirming the priority of God's grace.

Each practice reflects something of the full meaning of baptism, but each practice also risks the loss of part of that full meaning. The strength of infant baptism is that it bears powerful witness to the fact that God alone is the author of our salvation. It runs the risk, however, that people may minimize the individual decision of faith. The strength of believers' baptism is that it bears powerful witness to the need for an individual decision of faith. It runs the risk, however, that people may minimize the priority of God's grace and thus lapse into "works-righteousness," i.e., the idea that one's faith is a precondition for grace.

Whatever their practice, churches may lose sight of the responsibility placed upon the individual and the community by the act of baptism. Traditions practicing infant baptism may engage in an "indiscriminate baptism" in which the church does not take seriously the responsibility for nurturing baptized children to mature commitment in Christ. Traditions practicing believers' baptism are subject to a similar danger if baptism becomes a routine practice without authentic decision on the part of the child, adolescent, or adult. Traditions practicing believers' baptism have tended not to view children as a part of the church's membership and have, at times, not adequately recognized the church's responsibility to nurture unbaptized children toward the decision of faith. Traditions practicing infant baptism have, at times, understood the act as an elimination of original sin in such a way that the call to lifelong discipleship is weakened.

In light of the meaning of baptism, and considering the strengths and dangers of baptismal practices, we recognize that both infant and believers' baptism can be authentic practices in the one church of Jesus Christ. We affirm in line with the Disciples' tradition, that believers' baptism is, for us, the normative (standard) practice inasmuch as in this one act both God's gift of grace and the human response to that gift find focused expression. We likewise affirm that as baptism marks a new identity in Jesus Christ, whose ministry is that of self-giving service, so the baptized Christian enters into a life of self-giving service, and the church is called to nurture proper understandings and proper expressions of the manifold ethical dimensions of baptism.

Baptism has crucial significance for Christian conduct and obedience. In baptism, we died to sin and are raised to newness of life. Since we are dead to sin, we must not let sin reign in our bodies (Rom. 6:2–12). When we are baptized into Christ, we become members of a new community where God's righteousness reigns and the old distinctions which divide and disrupt human life are destroyed (Gal. 3:28). In baptism, we receive the gift of the Spirit, which empowers us to walk by the Spirit and bear the fruits of the Spirit (Gal. 5:22–25). In baptism we are united with Christ so as to share his suffering and participate in his ministry of obedient service. There is a great need in our era to rediscover the relationship between sacrament and service, between baptism and participation in God's mission in and for the world. As the World Council of Churches' *Baptism, Eucharist and Ministry* text puts it, baptism should not only call us to personal sanctification but should also "motivate Christians to strive for the realization of the will of God in all realms of life."

IV. Areas for Renewal and Growth in Disciples Theology and Practice of Baptism

In light of the preceding discussion on the nature and meaning of baptism, the Commission on Theology has identified three areas to which further attention needs to be given by Disciples in the future.

A. Rebaptism

The Commission on Theology endorses the ecumenical convergence regarding rebaptism which states that "baptism is administered only once" (COCU, VI, 12) and that congregations should avoid "any practice that could be interpreted as rebaptism" (BEM, "Baptism," 13). There are many reasons for such imperative language: (1) since baptism depends on God's grace and not simply on the "readiness" or "worthiness" of the person, rebaptism calls into question what God has done in that moment (whether or not we "remember" it); (2) rebaptism questions the sacramental integrity of other churches; (3) baptism marks incorporation into the one church and not simply into any one denomination; and, (4) baptism is not a momentary experience, but marks the beginning of a lifelong growth in Christ. It is important therefore, that baptism be "continually and responsibly reaffirmed" (COCU, VI,13).

The application of these principles becomes difficult for Disciples when an individual who has been baptized as an infant enters a new stage of faith and witness, and requests believers' baptism as the effective sign of renewal and commitment. A similar problem emerges when those who received believers' baptism become derelict and then return to the fold.

Genuine pastoral concern to give meaning and direction to the reconversion experience may be met in various ways other than repeating the baptismal sacrament. Reaffirmation of the baptismal faith is not a private affair, but includes the support and concern of the community of believers in response to the continuing manifestation of the abundant grace of God.

In many instances this may mean sharpening our awareness of the renewal that comes with participation in the Lord's Supper. Opportunity for rededication may be incorporated with the invitation to Discipleship following the sermon. In other instances, rejoining the fellowship of the committed is symbolized by receiving the "right hand of fellowship." Pastors and responsible persons and groups within each congregation (committees on worship, evangelism, etc.) may carefully assess how they reaffirm those who come from other churches and those who renew their commitment in service to God.

Various services for the renewal of baptismal faith are being developed around the country. These may be obtained from the Council on Christian Unity.

B. Baptism and the Meaning of Membership

Another issue which confronts Disciples is our pastoral responsibility to help all members to clarify our fundamental identity in Jesus Christ and to integrate the various meanings of church membership that impact our lives and witness:

- Christians are *members of a local congregation* which identify them with that particular fellowship and compel certain obligations for the care of that fellowship.
- Christians are *members of the global church* which calls for identification with people of diverse cultures, circumstances, ideologies and national interests. This identification also compels certain obligations to be informed about and share with the Christian family in its pluriform settings.
- Christians are *members of a rich heritage* reaching back through the history of the churches into biblical traditions all the way to creation, a heritage marked by both faithfulness and faithlessness in each generation. This identity compels certain obligations to know the contours of this heritage in appreciation for the pioneers of faith as well as guidance for our present context.
- Christians are *members of the unfolding drama of God's kingdom,* the lure of which constantly enables the individual to remold loyalties, values, and intentions. This identity compels an obligation to seek both justice and righteousness both as an individual and for the whole human community.

In baptism we are identified with the church local and global, past and future. From our baptism Christians grow through transformation of loyalties into citizenship of God's kingdom.

C. The Teaching of Baptism

It is hard to overemphasize the importance of effective instruction of the candidates for baptism. Such instruction, normally the responsibility of the local pastor, should deal with the meaning of baptism and its implications for the life of the candidate such as those addressed in this document.

What does it mean to accept the grace of God? What does it mean to be incorporated into the universal Church? Special attention should also be given to teaching in regard to the words of the baptismal service; for example, if the following service is used, attention should be given to such questions as: What does it mean to repent of sin and to renounce the false gods of this world? What does it mean to confess that Jesus is the Christ and to say that through baptism we participate in his death and resurrection? What does it mean to commit one's self to grow in a life of Christian discipleship? What does it mean to affirm that this service is not simply a human ceremony but an act of God?

These questions remind us that the themes and symbols of baptism take us to the very heart of the Christian faith. A baptism is, thus, an important teaching opportunity during which the whole community may be encouraged to deepen its understanding of what it means to be Christian.

In addition to adequate instruction for baptismal candidates, Disciples are becoming more aware that the preaching/teaching life of the church must include regular and intentional reminders about the meaning of baptism. In our baptism we were not only received into the family of God, but also ordained into the ministry of reconciliation. Therefore, continual reminders of this lifelong vocation, inaugurated at baptism, are needed to sustain our commitment and nourish us on the journey. The rich variety of imagery used by the New Testament writers to describe the meaning of baptism suggests abundant themes for educational settings in the church. Apart from the actual baptismal event, there are numerous other times within the life of the church for intentionally recalling our incorporation into the Body of Christ.

Celebration of Baptism

Introduction

Baptism, as the sacrament through which one is formally incorporated into the church, should be administered, whenever possible, during public worship (including the celebration of the Lord's Supper). This enables the members of the congregation to welcome the newly baptized person(s) into the body of Christ, to be reminded of their own baptismal vows, and to pledge themselves to be a community of continuing nurture.

The baptismal liturgy may come either (1) between the opening prayers and the proclamation of the Word through the reading of Scripture and preaching, or (2) between the sermon and the celebration of the Lord's Supper. The latter is theologically more appropriate, signifying that baptism is a response to the Word of God and an entry into the eucharistic community. The former has the practical advantage of allowing the newly baptized persons more time to dress before returning to the congregation to participate in the Lord's Supper.

The normal Disciples practice of assigning baptism to the pastor of the congregation is to be encouraged since such persons are set apart for representative, sacramental leadership, and they symbolize the universal connectedness of Christ's church. Few churches now contend, however, that the validity of baptism depends on the status of the celebrant. In situations where an ordained minister is unavailable, others (e.g., congregational elders) have authority to baptize.

Most orders of baptism (especially in this age of liturgical renewal throughout the church) include the following elements:

- a proclamation of Scripture(s) concerning baptism,
- an expression of repentance and a renunciation of evil,
- a profession of faith in Jesus Christ,
- an invocation of the Holy Spirit,
- the use of water (normally complete immersion in Disciples' practice),
- a declaration, following Matthew 28:19, that the baptism is administered in the name of the Trinity,
- expressions of welcome into the church.

The following order of service, based on the preceding theological discussion, is intended as but one possible model for use in the Christian Church (Disciples of Christ). The words of the service are said by the celebrating minister unless otherwise noted. The first three sections of the baptismal service should take place near the congregation—perhaps on the steps of the chancel—in order to underscore the participation and support of the worshiping community. Following the baptismal prayer, the congregation may sing a hymn or hymns as the celebrant and candidate(s) prepare for the actual baptism. It would be appropriate for the candidate(s) to be already robed, a sign of "putting on" a new life in Christ, during the first part of the liturgy. This would also make for a quicker transition to the baptistry. Otherwise, the candidate(s) will need to robe during the hymn.

Order of Service

Declaration of the Meaning of Baptism

[Refer to *Commentary Note* (1)]

Baptism is the sign of new life through Jesus Christ. Through baptism, we are brought into union with Christ and with his church around the world and across the ages. Through baptism, we participate in Christ's own death and resurrection. Through baptism we assume a new identity, committing ourselves to a life of love and righteousness.

As we approach this profound moment in the life of the church and of this [these] individual[s], let us remember the many dimensions of baptism revealed to us in Scripture:

"Do you now know that all of us who have been baptized into Christ Jesus were baptized into his death? We were buried therefore with him by baptism into death, so that as Christ was raised from the dead by the glory of the Father, we too might walk in newness of life" (Romans 6:3–4).

"For as many of you as were baptized into Christ have put on Christ. There is neither Jew nor Greek, there is neither slave nor free, there is neither male nor female; for you are all one in Christ Jesus" (Galatians 3:27–28).

"And Peter said to them, 'Repent, and be baptized every one of you in the name of Jesus Christ for the forgiveness of your sins; and you shall receive the gift of the Holy Spirit.

For the promise is to you and to your children and to all that are far off, every one whom the Lord our God calls [to him]'" (Acts 2:38–39).

Finally, we recall how Jesus Himself, baptized by John in the waters of the Jordan, commanded his followers to "make disciples of all nations, baptizing them in the name of the Father and of the Son and of the Holy Spirit" (Matthew 28:19).

II. Renunciation of Evil and Profession of Faith

[Refer to *Commentary Notes* (2)]

(The celebrant invites the person[s] [and their sponsors] to come forward.) _____N________, the community gathered here welcomes you with great joy to this holy celebration! Baptism is both God's gift and our human response to that gift. We pray for the transforming presence of God's Spirit and we ask that you respond to God's grace by repenting of your sins, by renouncing evil, by affirming your faith, and by committing yourself [selves] to grow in a life of Christian discipleship.

M: Do you repent of sin and earnestly pray for God's healing forgiveness?

B: I do.

M: Do you renounce being ruled by the false gods of this world—the snare of pride, the love of money, the power of violence?

B: I do [renounce them].

M: Do you, with Christians of every time and place, believe that "Jesus is the Christ, the Son of the Living God" (Matthew 16:16)?

B: I do [so believe].

M: Will you strive, with God's help, to follow Christ through faithful witness and loving service as part of his body, the church, all the days of your life [lives]?

B: I will [so strive].

M: Will you, the community here gathered, continue to uphold ____N_______ with your prayers and your witness in remembrance of your own baptism?

C: We will.

III. Baptismal Prayer

[Refer to *Commentary Notes* (3)]

Gracious God, we thank you that in every age you have made water a sign of your presence. In the beginning your Spirit brooded over the waters and they became the source of all creation. You led your people Israel through the waters of the Red Sea to their new land of freedom and hope. In the waters of the Jordan, your Son was baptized by John and anointed with your Spirit for his ministry of reconciliation. May this same Spirit bless the water we use today, that it may be a fountain of deliverance and new creation. Wash away the sins of those who enter it. Embrace them in the arms of your church. Pour out your Spirit on them that they may be ministers of reconciling love. Make them one with Christ, buried and raised in the power of his resurrection, in whose name we pray. Amen.

IV. Baptism

(The celebrant leads each candidate into the baptistry and lowers him or her backward into the water after saying the following words:)

By the authority of Jesus Christ, I baptize you, _____N_______, in the name of the Father and of the Son and of the Holy Spirit. Amen.

[Refer to Commentary Notes (4)]

V. Welcome

[Refer to *Commentary Notes* (5)]

(This may come immediately after the baptism or at the time of the Lord's Supper, at which those newly baptized should be specially served.)

M: ______N_______, God has blessed you with the Spirit and received you by baptism into the one, holy, catholic and apostolic church.

C: We welcome you into the bonds of Christian fellowship! Together, with Christians of all races and nations, we are members of Christ's body, united by Christ's blood into one family of faith.

M: Through baptism you have put on Christ, passing from darkness into light.

C: May you grow in the knowledge and love of God. May your faith shine as a light to the world.

Commentary Notes

The sequence suggested in this service calls for the first three sections to occur near the congregation, followed by a transition to the baptistry. Obviously there is nothing absolute about such a recommendation; such factors as architecture will (and should) play a role in determining what is most appropriate for each congregation. In some buildings the baptistry is so centrally located that the entire service could be conducted there without losing a sense of immediate community participation. Other pastors will want to move to the baptistry following the renunciation and confession in order that the prayer is said over the water itself. (In other churches the baptistry is separate from the sanctuary, making it difficult even to hold baptisms during regular Sunday worship.)

1. The opening lines of the "declaration" are drawn from the World Council of Churches' theological convergence document, *Baptism, Eucharist and Ministry* (BEM), paragraphs 2, 3, and 6 in the baptism section, and from the Consultation on Church Union's *COCU Consensus*, Chapter 6, paragraph 10. The major breakthrough represented by BEM may be the willingness of churches to acknowledge that the biblical witness regarding the meaning of baptism is richer than their separated traditions have taught. The passages used above lift up multiple images or meanings which yet point to a single reality.

Acts 2:38 and 2:39 have been used polemically by advocates of, respectively, believers' and infant baptism. They should be read together as a corrective to such polemics. The bracketed words in that passage are omitted for liturgical purposes in the *Inclusive Language Lectionary*.

2. The practice of sponsors, foreign to most Disciples, has much to commend it. These persons commit themselves to a special nurturing responsibility for the baptismal candidate,

thus signifying (a) the community's role in the response of faith and (b) the necessity of continual growth in faith after baptism.

The opening words of this section remind the candidate(s) and congregation that baptism is both a gift of grace and a response of faith, and prepare them for the questions that follow. The renunciation, focusing on contemporary forms of idolatry, is adapted from Max Thurian, "An Ecumenical Baptismal Liturgy," in *Baptism and Eucharist: Ecumenical Convergence in Celebration*. If the language of this renunciation seems too abstract ("the snare of pride, the love of money...") then it is possible to make it more direct (e.g., "Do you turn away from the false gods of this world—loving yourself more than God and neighbor, loving things more than God or each other,...").

The typical form of the Good Confession used in Disciples congregations is "Do you believe that Jesus is the Christ, the Son of the Living God, and do you take him as your Lord and Savior?" While such a formulation has the advantage of stating an intimate relationship between Jesus and the believer, it has at least two drawbacks: First, it opens the way for the saving work of Christ to be construed as an individualistic relationship with little regard for the corporate and cosmic dimensions of salvation. Second, it is the language of nineteenth-century revivalism and not of Scripture. Thus, it is recommended that the candidate(s) repeat Peter's simple confession as it appears in Matthew. Such a profession should be included in the baptismal liturgy in order not to separate the saving initiative of God through the Spirit from our personal appropriation of its benefits through trusting response.

Disciples insist that creeds articulated in the history of the church not be made "tests of fellowship" at the time of baptism. Persons come to this decision of faith, however, within the context of the Universal Church and of local communities whose faith is more fully developed than the simple confession of Peter. Thus, the candidate(s) might appropriately join with the whole congregation at some other point in the worship service in recitation of a broader confession of faith (especially the Apostles' Creed, a baptismal confession from the early church).

3. A prayer asking God to bless the water and recalling God's use of water in the history of salvation is standard in Roman Catholic and Anglican baptismal liturgies and is increasingly common among Protestants. As Keith Watkins points out, one reason for this prayer "is that it makes explicit that water is not the effective agent. Nor is the faith of the one being baptized. Nor is the power of the church what makes the change. Rather, God who is invoked in this prayer brings about the new birth" (unpublished manuscript). The strong emphasis in BEM on the activity of the Holy Spirit is, likewise, an affirmation that baptism is not a magic ritual (something we do) or a human initiation ceremony, but most fundamentally, an act of God.

4. There is objection in parts of the church to the masculine imagery of this traditional Trinitarian formula (from Matthew 28:19). There are also defenders who see "Father" as an intimate description of our relationship with God, given us by Jesus, and who regard its use in baptism as an expression of continuity with the apostolic church. The issue is a significant one and cannot be resolved in this service. It is important to remember, however, that substitute formulas may raise other problems, and that all human language about God is symbolic and must be used carefully.

5. The welcome described in this section is a focused, public expression of the informal and nonliturgical welcome normally extended by Disciples of congregations following the worship service.

Some Disciples congregations are discovering that various symbolic acts, such as the anointing with oil as a sign of the gift of the Spirit or the giving of a candle as a sign of passing from darkness into light, can reinforce the significance of the ceremony as well as give powerful expression to its meaning. Other congregations extend "the right hand of fellowship" as a gesture of welcome into this community of faith.

Members of the Commission on Theology

William R. Baird	Walter D. Bingham
Paul A. Crow, Jr.	James Duke
Wallace R. Ford	H. Jackson Forstman, *Chairperson*
Beverly R. Gaventa	Howard B. Goodrich, Jr.
Kenneth E. Henry	Joe R. Jones
Michael Kinnamon	Vance Martin
Narka Ryan	Ann Updegraff Spleth
Clark M. Williamson	Robert K. Welsh *(Staff)*

Questions for Reflection and Discussion

1. Read or review sections I, II, and III. From the scriptural texts given and the history provided, how do you understand infant baptism and believers' baptism? In what ways have you experienced each of these baptisms? How do you see the usage of two types of baptisms to be a stumbling block to ecumenism? How do you see it as a potential benefit?
2. Read or review "Rebaptism" in section IV. As you consider the arguments against rebaptism, how would you respond to a 45-year-old seeking to be rebaptized? She was baptized as a ten-year-old child, left the church in her twenties, and has recently become a spiritual leader in the church.
3. If possible, go to the place where your faith community holds baptisms. Invite those who plan worship to participate in this session. Reenact a typical baptism. How do the elements included or excluded compare to those listed in the example "Order of Service"?
4. The second commentary note (p. 128) suggests using sponsors for baptismal candidates. Has your congregation used sponsors or mentors? Why or why not? What could you do to encourage the practice of using sponsors or mentors? Consider using Prepare the Way, a membership preparation curriculum that integrates the use of mentors.
5. Review the words about the Good Confession, discussed in the second commentary note (p. 129). Consider

together the theological concerns mentioned. Would you change the Good Confession to more accurately depict the believer's role in the community of faith? If so, how? Of the statements listed in part II of the "Order of Service" (p. 126), which ones does your congregation use? Do you have others? What affirmations or changes do you sense calling your group to suggest in the celebration of baptism in worship? How will you educate the congregation about these changes?

6. For a contemporary and historic look at Disciple thought and practice of baptism, refer to *Baptism and Belonging,* listed in the bibliography.
7. For further study on baptism, refer to *Baptism, Embodiment of the Gospel: Disciples Baptismal Theology* by Clark Williamson, listed in the bibliography as part of the Nature of the Church Series.

A Word to the Church on the Lord's Supper (1991)

In its major study on the nature of the Church within the tradition of the Christian Church (Disciples of Christ), the Commission on Theology has sent reports to the General Assembly, the regions, and the congregations on the themes of ecclesiology (1979), mission (1981), authority (1983), ministry (1985), and baptism (1987). These reports, and the study books published by Christian Board of Publication on the same themes, constitute an important body of theological literature among the Disciples in the last decades of the 20th century. Over the past two years (1989–1991) the Commission explored the theology and practice of the Lord's Supper. Their report to the Tulsa General Assembly (1991) identifies some of the essential meanings of the Eucharist and some of the practices that require thoughtful reflection by the whole church, especially the congregations.

I. Introduction

"As members of the Christian Church, We confess that… At the table of the Lord we celebrate with thanksgiving the saving acts and presence of Christ." These words in the Preamble to *The Design for the Christian Church (Disciples of Christ)* remind us of the significance of the Lord's Supper in Christian worship. The affirmation that the church today, as in apostolic times, is called to gather at the Lord's Table on the first day of the week has been a prominent and enduring feature of Disciples church life. Indeed, it is a mark of our identity as a church. As Disciples, we recognize that the Lord's Supper is a means by which we are nourished by the love of God in Jesus Christ and through that love are made one with one another and with the Church Universal.

That this is the significance of the Lord's Supper is a truth that Disciples are made aware of perhaps more surely by our partaking of the Supper than by any statements we make about it. Who of us has not experienced at the Table the reality of God's good news and of our oneness in Christ so deeply and intensely that the words we use to speak of it seem to fall short of their mark? The Lord's Supper means more than the church is ever quite able to say about it.

The sense that the Lord's Supper is an act of inexhaustible spiritual richness is one that Disciples share in common with Christians of all times and places. The accounts of the Lord's Supper and the references to its observance recorded in the New Testament indicate how many powerful meanings it conveyed to early Christians. The desire to celebrate and express the Table's significance for the church has led faithful Christians over the centuries to develop a wide variety of forms of worship, devotional meditations, and formulations of doctrine.

As Disciples we too join with the Church Universal in seeking to acknowledge the significance of the Lord's Supper in ways that are in keeping with the witness of Scripture, with the God-given unity of all Christians, and with the love of God for all the world. We too wish to make it known by all we say and do with respect to the Table that God's Good news in Jesus Christ is at the very heart of our faith and our calling as a church.

For precisely this reason, how we celebrate the Lord's Supper (Eucharist, Holy Communion) and what we teach about it are never to be taken for granted. These are matters deserving thoughtful consideration and reconsidered ever and again. Like all Christians, Disciples are led to ask and to respond to a question of faith: are our worship practices, our teachings, and our theological reflections adequate testimonies to the significance of the Lord's Supper?

This question arose early on in the Campbell-Stone movement. It was given thoughtful consideration then, and at other times in our church's history. Concern for the vitality of our worship and dedication to the cause of Christian unity gives the Disciples good reason to reconsider the question once again. The Theology Commission of the Council on Christian Unity, Christian Church (Disciples of Christ) offers the thoughts which follow as an aid for reflection and a stimulus for further study and conversation within the Christian Church (Disciples of Christ).

II. The Disciples Heritage

Early Disciples teaching and practice regarding the Lord's Supper were very much bound up with the situation of the churches at the turn of the nineteenth century. The ties can be said to have been both negative and positive. On the negative side were "protests" on the part of the Campbell-Stone movement against what were perceived as mistaken or inappropriate views of the Lord's Supper current among Christians of the day, Protestant and Catholic alike. On the positive side were proposals for "a new reformation" of doctrine and practice. The protest as well as the proposals grew out of commitments to the very same principles to which the traditions of the churches claimed to be beholden, foremost among them the authority of the biblical witness to the faith and order of the apostolic church.

The protests of the early Disciples were directed against any and every view of the Lord's Supper judged to be at variance with its significance for the church. They objected when it seemed: (1) that the act of communion was viewed as if it were a human work performed in order to earn God's favor or an activity that dispensed its spiritual benefits apart from faith; (2) that preaching alone, or perhaps some private experience of the Holy Spirit working within the soul, was viewed as a substitute for weekly observance of the Supper; and (3) that the churches taught their creeds, theologies, and orders of ministry in ways that hindered Christians from gathering at the Table.

The varied protests were at root the same. Disciples did not want Christians to forget that the Lord's Supper is a means by which God's people are nourished by the love of God in Jesus Christ and through that love are made one with one another and with the Church Universal.

The essence of their proposals for reform was, as Alexander Campbell put it, that "faith is then the PRINCIPLE, and ordinances the MEANS, of all spiritual enjoyment; because all the wisdom, power, love, mercy, compassion, or GRACE OF GOD is in the ordinances of the Kingdom of Heaven; and if all grace be in them it can only be enjoyed through them." (*Christian System,* 5th ed., pp. 148–49). Elsewhere he stated, "the current reformation if conspicuous now or hereafter for any thing, must be so because of the conspicuity it gives the Bible and its ordinances as the indispensable moral means of spiritual life and health." (*Millennial Harbinger* [January 1843, p. 9]).

By the term "ordinance" Campbell referred to "commemorative" or "monumental" institutions which were appointed—ordained—by God to be perpetual declarations of God's saving action in Jesus Christ on behalf of sinful creatures. Each ordinance served to convey "a special grace peculiar to itself; so that no one can be substituted for another, or neglected, without the lack, or loss, of the blessing in the Divine will and grace connected with it." (*Millennial Harbinger* [December 1855, p. 678]). One such ordinance was the Lord's Supper; its "special grace" is that of nourishing, strengthening, and hence perfecting the faith and unity of baptized believers gathered in worship.

To speak of the Lord's Supper as an "ordinance" by which Christians declare and enjoy the grace of God, as Campbell and those who followed him and Stone did, was to deal with terms and to address issues which were, and still are, commonplaces of theological discussion. How to identify, to conduct, and to give a theological account of acts such as Baptism and the Lord's Supper which, as "visible signs of an invisible grace," are called "the sacraments" of the church have been topics of concern throughout history. What early Disciples had to say about these matters were variations on themes especially well known to and often debated by members of the extended family of the Reformed churches, rooted in the Reformation led by John Calvin and others.

These debates, and even more the divisions they occasioned, led Campbell and others to shy away from the word "sacrament" and other terms associated with issues of theological controversy. Conformity to biblical precedent and language, they maintained, was the best means by which to restore the church to health, peace, and unity. Yet in fact the word "ordinance" was not itself a biblical term; it appeared in the Westminster Confession and in Reformed theology generally as a synonym for "sacrament." In short, early Disciples drew upon the resources of Scripture and Tradition alike in order to direct the churches to worship practices and teachings which would do justice to the fundamental theological significance of the Lord's Supper.

In their own worship, early Disciples clearly granted the Lord's Supper the special status as a visible sign and seal of God's grace, a status traditionally termed "sacramental." In light of apostolic precedent, they regarded its celebration to be the one essential act of Sunday worship; congregations gathered at the Table even when they had no one available to preach a sermon. Insistence upon weekly communion made the Disciples a peculiar household among nineteenth-century Christians. It made them seem more in tune with the wishes of such Reformed leaders as John Calvin than were those who avowed a strict "Calvinism," and at the same time more in line with the emphases of "catholic" and "sacramental" churches (Roman Catholic, Anglican-Episcopalian, and Eastern Orthodox) than of their Protestant kin. In addition, in permitting each congregation to worship with due regard for reverence, decency, and good order but without reliance upon a standardized liturgy, they seemed to be decidedly "free church" reformers.

III. Orientation to the Theological Reflection

The strengths of this mix of resources—biblical, Catholic, Protestant, and "free"—have been amply displayed throughout the course of Disciples history. Weekly observance of the Lord's Supper in particular, and with it an awareness of the "centrality of communion" in worship, has proved of inestimable value to us. It has served to keep us mindful of the Gospel and of our oneness in Christ even when all else may have seemed to fail. Realizing its value, this practice is one which Disciples may rightly prize for our own church and heartily commend to others in our ecumenical dialogues and relationships.

By the same token, this mix of resources must, like any other, be responsibly tended. Concerned to express the significance of the Lord's Supper, the churches have given careful attention to their forms of worship. For the same reason they have also developed theological accounts, i.e., doctrines (teachings), of what takes place at the Table. A wide variety of such doctrines in found in the creeds, the confessions, and the theological works of the churches.

These doctrines are basically, like all theological efforts, examples of faith seeking understanding. They are intended to remind members of the church that in the Lord's Supper, as in baptism, there is a connection between the visible signs of the rite and the invisible, spiritual reality they signify, as well as a vital relationship between the rite itself and the benefits it offers to faithful participants. This connection and this relationship are always, and inevitably, discussed in works of church theology dealing with the Lord's Supper.

Unfortunately, the doctrines of the Lord's Supper developed by churches have all too often led to confusion rather than edification, to discord and even division rather than peace and unity, to exclusivistic and sometimes arrogant dealings with Christians of differing views. The impulse to avoid the harmful effects of theology is deep and strong in the Disciples heritage. Disciples refuse to treat any doctrine or "theory" of the Lord's Supper as a "test of fellowship," that is, as a justification for denying sincere and otherwise worthy Christians the right to partake of the sacrament or for barring the way to Christian unity.

This is a healthy impulse, rooted as it is in an awareness that the Lord's Supper is a God-given means for enlivening Christian faith and promoting Christian reconciliation. Thus it becomes all the more regrettable when this impulse too—no less than officially authorized statements of doctrine—leads to mistaken views that harm the church: for example, that Disciples simply do not care if people believe anything, or nothing, with respect to the meaning of the Lord's Supper, or that we need not bother to give any theological account of our practices, or that each congregation may say and do whatever it pleases in worship, with no concern for questions of theology.

Faithfulness to Scripture, respect for the resources of our church's history, concern for the vitality of our corporate worship, and commitment to the cause of Christian unity require us to teach what we, as Disciples, understand the significance of the Lord's Supper to be. We are also to address, in light of this understanding, the various issues related to the form of our worship which are raised in our local churches and our ecumenical involvements.

IV. Biblical—The Theological Meanings of the Lord's Supper

In what is said and done at the Lord's Supper Christians have the opportunity to experience an extraordinary array and richness of meanings. The traditional English terms used for the rite highlight a number of its key characteristics: it is the Lord's Supper (1 Cor. 11:20), but also the Eucharist ("thanksgiving"), "Holy Communion" (1 Cor. 10:16), "the Breaking of the Bread" (Acts 2:42, Lk.24:35), and the Mass (beginning with the dismissal of those preparing for baptism and concluding with the sending out of baptized believers into the world for Christian service). But these names are neither a clear nor full indication of its manifold and multi-layered meaning. Disciples attentive to the witness of the New Testament will not fail to acknowledge and to reflect upon at least five strands of meaning woven together in the liturgy.

1. Remembrance: As Paul recounts the tradition known to him, he speaks of remembrance: "This do in remembrance of me" (1 Cor. 11:23–26). The Greek term used here, *anamnesis,* certainly involves memory, but it carries special force. It is not merely a recollection of something long gone and hence remote from us, but a re-presentation which makes what is past a vivid and lively reality here and now. Jesus Christ himself with all he has accomplished for us and for all creation is present in this *anamnesis.*

In remembering as *anamnesis* we go beyond thinking of an event that took place in bygone days. Through this joyful celebration God's saving acts and promises in Jesus Christ are re-called from the past; they are brought before our hearts and minds with stark immediacy. A Spiritual coming down from Black Christian tradition captures this meaning well: in asking "were you there when they crucified my Lord," the answer "yes" is already given.

And so it is that in reenacting the Lord's Supper the line dividing past and present is erased. We become eyewitnesses of, indeed participants in, the event. The passion of Jesus Christ, "for the remission of sins," is re-presented to us. We join the company of disciples, i.e., the followers of Christ of every time and place, who gather to share this meal with him. To "remember" the occasion in which God's covenant of love was renewed is to share in the renewal of that covenant. The Supper strengthens us, and all who partake of it, for our life-journeys of discipleship.

2. Communion of the Faithful: The Lord's Supper is a time of communion *(koinonia)*. We commune with Jesus Christ and with all others who follow him. Here our Savior is present with us. For centuries Christians have debated about how to describe and explain the character of his presence, and Disciples certainly vary in their understandings of it. What we hold in common with all Christian traditions is that at the Table we encounter the Risen Christ.

We most often speak of this communion in quite simple terms. The Table is not ours, but the Lord's. Christ Jesus is the host; it is he who invites us to be guests at this meal, to sup and commune with him. Likewise, when we gather, we commune not only with him but with all those who have responded to his invitation. We are brought into a spiritual unity with all Christians, not only those with us at that very moment but with those of all times and all places.

3. Sacrifice. That the passion of Christ is a sacrifice offered up for the forgiveness of sins is a theme that has been important to Christians from the earliest church to today. It has been variously interpreted, and some of these interpretations have given rise to a great deal of controversy. Within the Protestant heritage, for example, there has been strong opposition to the view that those who preside at the Table are to carry the title of priests, i.e., those who offer up sacrifices, and that they act in order to repeat Christ's sacrifice again and again.

For disciples, heirs of the Protestant Reformation, the meaning of the sacrifice at the Table is understood primarily in the sense that we commemorate the unique sacrifice made once and for all by Jesus Christ himself. Among the many insights conveyed to us by this theme, three are especially important.

First, a great price has been paid for us, for the remission of our sins and for our salvation. We are neither required nor even able to do anything to add to what Jesus has already done. The work of Christ is a grace, an undeserved gift, freely offered to us. Second, it is not presiding officers of the ceremony but the whole people of God who, in response to the sacrifice of Christ, offer up our own sacrifices of praise and thanksgiving, a giving of ourselves to God who brings good news to sinners. Third, by the sacrificial life and death of Jesus, our own lives are given new direction: we are called to self-giving service for the sake of the church and of the whole of God's creation.

4. Unity. The Lord's Supper signifies that the unity of all believers in Christ is at once a reality and a goal yet to be attained. The founders of the Disciples, notably Alexander Campbell and Barton Warren Stone, reminded their followers that the communion service demonstrated that the oneness of all believers was a fact. As worshippers receive bread from one loaf, broken for them, and share from one cup, poured for them, they are knit together in one body, in one faith, in one Lord and Savior.

They also taught that the Lord's Supper was a powerful means by which Christians of various traditions and theological views might come to a heightened awareness of and commitment to the unity of all. Further, in the struggle which led Disciples to affirm open communion, welcoming to the Table all followers of Christ regardless of denominational and creedal affiliation, a profound sense of the unity of the church is expressed.

5. The Feast of the Reign of God. At the Lord's Table we proclaim Jesus Christ "until he comes." This phrase is one of many in Scripture pointing us toward the future, toward Christ's coming again (cf. Mt. 26:20, 1 Cor. 11:26). The Lord's Supper is an anticipation, and indeed a foretaste, of the joyful festal meal celebrating this momentous event. It calls us forward to the time when God's will for the whole of creation will be accomplished and God's reign will come in its fullness and perfection. It directs us toward that age when we live together, as God would have us do, in justice, harmony, peace, and joy.

This sign of the future cannot fail but make us painfully aware that at present we and the world we live in are far from what God intends for the creation. We realize that many sisters and brothers are not present with us at the Table, and how many living under conditions of poverty, injustice, and oppression will go without any meal at all to nourish them.

To partake of the Lord's Supper is to experience a new and confident hope in God's ultimate victory over evil. With this hope comes a mandate to care for the well-being of the world and all its inhabitants. Jesus ate with publicans and notorious sinners, and instructed his followers to care for the poor, the needy, the outcasts, and those who are "the least" in the eyes of the world. Thus the foretaste of joy which we experience at the Table is not only a comfort to us but a challenge. It prepares us to undertake our mission of witness and service in the world.

Although these five themes certainly do not exhaust the full meaning of the Lord's Supper, they convey messages too important to be neglected in the worship and teaching of our church. Each and every one of them deserves to be included in our communion services, in our preaching, and in our teaching of the faith.

It is also important for Disciples to give thought to the distinctive status and character of the Lord's Supper in the Christian community. The sacraments of the church are God-given means for the proclamation of the gospel which come down to us from the apostolic witness to Jesus Christ. Unlike other forms of proclamation such as preaching, they are not only a telling of the gospel story and its meaning but are a visible and tangible enactment of the gospel. Here words, actions, and physical elements combine to disclose God's gracious love in Jesus Christ.

God's gracious love has been and is revealed on earth through physical media: in the incarnation, by the humanity of Jesus; in baptism, by water; in the Lord's Supper, by bread and wine. In the Lord's Supper, these quite ordinary material elements necessary to sustain life are distributed to and received by the participants, and consumed. Partaking of the one bread and the common cup becomes, by God's grace, the occasion for spiritual nourishment and renewal of faith. By this sign, made in conjunction with prayers and the unfailing use of the words of institution, the reality of God's gracious love in Jesus Christ is signified and experienced anew.

The reality is all-embracing; it encompasses the past, present, and future. In the Lord's Supper the dimensions of time come to a point of convergence. The death and resurrection of Jesus are recalled (1 Cor. 11:23–25) and the coming Christ (1 Cor. 11:26) is anticipated in the midst of the experience of the presence of the risen Christ among his people (Lk. 24:30–31).

Precisely because the reality of divine grace in Jesus Christ is not only signified but thereby experienced anew in the Lord's Supper, the bread and the wine are by no means "mere" or "empty" signs which give rise by free association to various subjective feelings and thoughts within those who partake of them. What occurs is a communion with Jesus Christ, who is also present, with the faithful, as host and as redemptive power.

His presence is not physical as in his earthly life; nor do the bread and the wine change their material properties or become something other than signs. Yet the connection between the signs and the reality they signify and the vital relationship between the rite itself and the benefits it conveys to those who receive it in faith are such that Christians rightly proclaim that Jesus Christ, who was crucified and raised from the dead, is with us at the Table.

V. Issues of Practice

In light of all that we know and may still learn of the significance of the Lord's Supper, Disciples no less than other churches have cause to consider the adequacy of our worship practices. Both our actions and our words are to draw those who commune into the enlarged sphere of meaning which the service opens up and to encourage receptivity to the rich spiritual benefits it makes available.

"Free church" worship such as ours, which does not rely on a standardized liturgy, provides us the opportunity to express our faith and to refresh our worship by judiciously drawing upon the resources to be found in Scripture, the Christian Tradition, and contemporary life. Theologically thoughtful uses of this freedom direct us to seek out forms of language and practice that affirm continuity with historic patterns of apostolic, Protestant, Catholic, and Orthodox worship, even as they reflect the best of contemporary insights into the meaning of Christian faith in our times. Particularly worthy of commendation as a resource for celebrating the Lord's Supper is the Disciples work *Thankful Praise: A Resource for Christian Worship* (edited by Keith Watkins [St. Louis: CBP Press, 1987]).

Several issues, however, are in need of careful study and further reflection by Disciples today. Among them are these:

1. The Word and the Sacrament of the Lord's Supper. In the Protestant tradition, the Lord's Supper is always to be celebrated within the context of the corporate worship of the faithful in which the Word of God revealed in scripture is read, its meaning(s) explicated in preaching, and then proclaimed in the prayers and actions at the Table. These are concerns that deserve emphasis, lest the Lord's Supper be mistaken for an act of personal religiosity or corrupted by subjective feelings and thoughts unrelated to its central focus, which is the Gospel concerning Jesus Christ.

The Sunday worship of Disciples congregations follows the pattern of joining Word and Sacrament. On occasion, however, the Lord's Supper is observed as a separate form of worship, often at the close of some special gathering or meeting. In such cases there is always opportunity to hold Word and Sacrament together, and this should be done. In offering an invitation to commune, a prayer of thanksgiving, or a meditation, the scriptural message of the communion service may be recounted and reflected upon.

2. The Place of the Lord's Supper in the Order of Worship. Attention needs to be given to the place of the Supper in the order of worship. Disciples in their freedom have followed various customs.

It seems that in the early years of our history the Lord's Supper was generally placed at the conclusion, as the climax, of Sunday worship, in keeping with the worship traditions of most churches. Later in the nineteenth century, however, many American churches were led, for various reasons, to place the sermon after the Lord's Supper; many Disciples congregations adopted this custom. The sermon, preached by one individual, and the response to it by individuals making a public confession of faith became the climax of worship, in place of the action of the community gathered around the Table as a corporate body.

Whatever its values may be, this custom has the effect of elevating the pulpit over the Table by making the Lord's Supper preparatory to the sermon. It runs counter to the practice in the history of worship since apostolic times. The reading and preaching of the Word of God calls forth among those who worship a decision for or rededication to the life of faith. Thereafter, the faithful approach the Table to make and receive a sign and seal of the Gospel, to commune with the Savior Christ Jesus and all of his disciples, and to receive from this spiritual food new strength and vitality for undertaking our calling of Christian service in the world. Thus the Lord's Supper is the fitting climax to our public worship.

3. The Invitation to Communion. Jesus Christ himself invites his disciples to his Table. The invitation offered by our worship leader(s) serves only to make Christ's call known. Many churches have at some time in the past—and even now at present—made a conscious attempt to restrict the invitation to those who are deemed "qualified" to participate.

The use of creeds and other specifically denominational criteria for this purpose has been challenged and set aside by Disciples. Thus it is our custom as a community of faith to invite all baptized Christians to partake of the Lord's Supper with us.

Here, however, two points are to be recalled. The first is that each of the church's sacraments has a special character as well as a special benefit all its own. Baptism is a sign and seal of our incorporation into the body of Christ; the Lord's Supper is a sign and seal of the spiritual nourishment we receive as members of that body. Hence it is for Christians, as members of the body of Christ through baptism (whatever its form), that the Table is intended.

The second point, related and critical to our understanding of the first, is this. It is not ours to investigate and decide, as though the judgment were our own, who is and is not truly a follower of Christ worthy to come to the Table with us. This is a matter of faith, and conscience, beyond our reckoning. As Disciples, we invite anyone of sincere faith who wills to come to the Table, for we believe that we no less than others are offered there mercy, forgiveness, and new life.

4. Confession of Sin and Absolution. The path to the Lord's Table is marked by an awareness of our utter unworthiness of the love of God. Christians find that our experience and measure of understanding of this love as a forgiving love are made powerful when we confess our sins, as individuals and as a community, and hear God's Word of acceptance. To drink worthily of the cup filled with Christ's blood poured out for the remission of sins, we drink repentantly, with humility and with thanksgiving. Hence the opportunity to confess our sins and to hear the promise of their forgiveness in Jesus Christ is essential in our worship. Indeed, without forgiveness there are some who will never feel themselves worthy to partake of the Supper. Provision for the confession of sins and for words of assurance may be made, whether by corporate statements or by prayers early in the worship service or as the community prepares to come to the Table

5. The Question of Presidency. Who is to preside at the Lord's Supper is another of the important issues to be dealt with by Disciples today. Various customs and views can be found among us. There is widespread acknowledgment that the elders, now by and large understood to be "lay (non-ordained) officers" of the congregation, are to play a prominent role at the Table, offering prayers and in some cases proclaiming the words of institution. They are generally but by no means always joined by the ordained minister, who may or may not preside. Regrettably, in some cases the minister is excluded from serving, much less presiding, at the Table.

Leadership at the Table is not a prerogative given to an ordained minister alone, but it is a responsibility shared by the ministers and elders of the congregation, and by other church members whom the congregation authorizes to serve the community in this role. This is a conviction for which sound theological and practical reasons can be given. But often discussions and practices regarding the roles of the elders and the minister reflect misunderstandings of our heritage.

This is especially true in any case of the exclusion of the minister from any leadership role in the administration of the Lord's Supper. First of all, the office of elder spoken of by Alexander Campbell, Barton Warren Stone, and other early Disciples was understood to be one carried out by those who were duly appointed and fully recognized as the ministers of the church. It was an ordained office, in that ordination was the formal ceremony that confirmed appointment and recognition. The current arrangement in which there is an ordained minister and several "lay" elders developed only gradually thereafter, as ordination became granted ever more increasingly to elders—and evangelists—with a gift (and/or formal theological education) for preaching, teaching, and pastoral oversight.

Even today elders are appointed by our congregations to a ministry of congregational oversight, including service at the Lord's Table. This is a form of ministry even if it is not any longer understood to bear all the responsibilities of ordained ministry or formally acknowledged by an act of ordination.

Second, Disciples follow the Protestant tradition generally in emphasizing the importance of the priesthood of all believers. Our heritage affirms that all believers are eligible, by virtue of their baptism, to be chosen by the church to serve at the Table. The "priesthood" belongs to the people, the *laos* (laity, the people) of God. It is by the church's choosing that one or more of their number may lead them in worship, whether or not a formal service such as ordination is held to confirm that appointment.

Precisely for these reasons, however, the ordained minister of the congregation is not to be denied a role in administering the Lord's Supper. This practice fails to recall that the ordained minister is an elder of the church, charged with and appointed for its pastoral leadership. To refuse to allow the minister to serve at the Table is to deny the collegiality of pastors and elders.

Ordained ministers are also part of the laos, the people, and hence they too can be appointed to serve at the Table. And indeed they serve in many ways as the representatives of the whole people of God. Among Disciples as well as in ecumenical settings the ordained ministry is often referred to as a representative ministry. Thus it is altogether appropriate for the ordained minister to offer or to lead the congregation in offering the words of institution. Given our commitment to the cause of Christian unity, selecting the ordained minister to preside at the Table is of special importance: Those who lead us in our worship at the Table do so by appointment, and ordination is the most universally acknowledged act by which the churches formally mark such appointment to their public, representative ministries.

6. Prayers at the Table. Communion prayers, however many are offered, should include as a basic element the offering of thanksgiving. Christians here express gratitude for God's love, for the life and death of Jesus Christ, and for the gift of salvation. At this time the meaning of

Communion as Eucharist, thanksgiving, is expressed with special poignancy.

The prayers at the Table are also to include a petition calling for the presence of the Holy Spirit, through whose power the bread and wine provide spiritual nourishment for the refreshing of our faith, the upbuilding of the body of Christ, and our living as faithful servants of Jesus Christ in the world. This part of the prayer is often called the invocation or the *epiclesis,* both words meaning "to call upon." It is also appropriate in communion prayers to focus on our remembrance of the sacrifice of Jesus Christ, our anticipation of God's ultimate victory, our awareness of the presence of Jesus Christ among us, and our appreciation for the richness of meaning conveyed by the Lord's Supper.

In many churches, and many Disciples congregations, the Lord's Prayer is included in the liturgy of the Table. It is a way by which the entire congregation may be prepared for and drawn into what takes place when we partake of the Supper. In the worship of Disciples, the Lord's Prayer most naturally comes after an invitation to communion or in the context of a communion meditation.

7. The Words of Institution. The unfailing use of the biblical words of institution in the Lord's Supper focuses our devotions on the significance of the sacrament. It is also a testimony to our unity with all Christians of all times and in all places, for no specific act of worship is more universally observed by Christians than this. The words are those of Scripture (Mt. 26:26–29, Mk. 14:22–25, Lk.22:14–19, or 1 Cor. 11:23–26), each and every one of which is a capsule summary of the primary theological meanings of the Supper. Repeating those words time after time makes it known that what we do here is not ordinary eating and drinking, but a sharing with Jesus Christ and with the whole community of faith in the meal that celebrates and communicates the Gospel.

8. Elements and Actions of the Lord's Supper. Disciples, like Protestants generally and following the lead of Alexander Campbell in particular, are well aware that the elements and actions of the Lord's Supper are "symbolic," and tend to view them in rather rationalistic terms. But the Protestant heritage and Campbell himself had an appreciation of the import and power of living symbols more keen than that customary among Disciples today.

It is to be recalled that how we conduct the Lord's Supper may have the effect of heightening or diminishing our experience of its meanings. We would do well to set aside the sterile practice of using tiny, individual, and pre-cut pieces of bread and little cups of juice or wine in favor of loaves of bread that can be broken in the sight of all the congregation and cups that can be filled and then shared either by dipping or sipping.

At the very least, and as Campbell advocated, we should allow believers to see a loaf of bread "significantly" broken as the scriptural words of institution are spoken. Likewise, as worshippers hear the words "poured out for you," they are to see the fruit of the vine being poured out into a chalice from which they are to partake. There is to be a discernible relationship between what is said and what is done by symbolic action at the Table.

The use of a loaf of bread (whether leavened or unleavened) and of a significant amount of wine or grape juice is a visible and tangible reminder that God's self-revelation occurs in and through earthly media. God condescends to meet us where we are, on earth, and as we are, creatures who are taught and powerfully moved by our sensory experiences. When at the Lord's Supper the breaking of bread the pouring of wine, and the sharing together of food that sustains us are joined with God's Word of Good News and the power of the Spirit, we are nourished by the love of God in Jesus Christ and through that love are made one with another and with the Church Universal.

Members of the Commission on Theology

William R. Baird	Walter D. Bingham
Paul A. Crow, Jr.	James O. Duke
Wallace Ford	Jack Forstman, *Chairperson*
Beverly Gaventa	Richard L. Harrison, Jr.

Kenneth Henry	Joe R. Jones
Michael Kinnamon	Vance Martin
Eleanor Scott Meyers	Narka Ryan
Clark K. Williamson	

Questions for Reflection and Discussion

1. After reviewing the history of Disciples theology and practice of the Lord's Supper, which of those beliefs and practices have endured to the present?
2. How do you understand the difference between *ordinance* and *sacrament*?
3. In section V, "Issues of Practice," consider with the worship planners of your faith community each of the issues listed. How does the practice and understanding of worship in your faith community compare to the ideas presented by the commission?
4. Invite those responsible for planning worship in your faith community to articulate the theological suppositions and experiences that inform their planning of worship for the local faith community. If worship planning is largely based on local precedence and preference, how can it be helped to reflect with greater integrity the faith and practice of the whole church?
5. For further study of the Lord's Supper, refer to *The Lord's Supper* by James O. Duke and Richard L. Harrison, listed in the bibliography as part of the Nature of the Church Series.

Glossary

Council of Constantinople: an ecumenical council in A.D. 381 that affirmed and enlarged the faith as expressed in the Nicene Creed and clarified such important teachings as the nature of the Trinity, the divinity of the Holy Spirit, the human and divine natures of Jesus Christ, and the status of the Church of Constantinople (Orthodox) as second only to Rome.

Discernment: a process of gaining insight or making a decision. The following discernment process was listed in the "Guidelines for Group Discernment" in the 1997 General Assembly *Business Docket and Program* (90).

- Seek God's intentions for the church with earnestness.
- Cultivate an attitude of humility which recognizes our human limitations and sinfulness.
- Pray patiently regarding the issue at hand.
- Attend actively to each persons' words, feelings, and non-verbal expressions in the spirit of genuine caring.
- Recognize and release preconceived perceptions.
- Open the heart and mind to new insights, feelings, and points of view.
- Take responsibility for one's own feelings, words, and actions as individual members of Christ's body.
- Speak honestly about what is perceived to be God's unfolding intentions for the church and world.

Ecumenical council: assemblies of leaders of the church throughout the world whose decisions on Christian doctrine, worship, and practice are accepted and received with great reverence for Christian faith and living. The decisions of these councils are considered authoritative only if they are in harmony with God's Word. The first seven councils are called "ecumenical" (from the Greek word *Oikoumene*) because their decisions are believed to represent Christians "throughout the whole inhabited world."

Grace: the free and unearned gift of God's love and help.

Holy: related to or deriving from God; set apart for God's use or service.

Nicene Creed: an expression of the essentials of the Christian faith resulting from the ecumenical council of Nicea (in Asia Minor) in A.D. 325 and modified in 381:

> *We believe in one God, the Father Almighty, maker of all things visible and invisible, and in one Lord, Jesus Christ, the Son of God, the only-begotten of the Father, that is, of the substance of the Father, God from God, light from light, true God from true God, begotten, not made, of one substance with the Father, through whom all things were made, those things that are in heaven and those things that are on earth, who for us men and for our salvation came down and was made flesh, suffered, rose again on the third day, ascended into the heavens, and will come to judge the living and the dead.*
>
> *I believe in the Holy Ghost, the Lord, the Giver of Life, who proceedeth from the Father, who with the Father and the Son together is worshiped and glorified, who spake by the prophets. And I believe in one Catholic and Apostolic Church. I acknowledge one baptism for the remission of sins. And I look for the resurrection of the dead, and the life of the world to come.*

Sanctification: for Christians, the fact of our having been made ready to receive and to share God's love and help.

Shalom: the Hebrew word for peace; wholeness, the fulfillment of God's justice.

Bibliography

Beazley, George G., Jr., *The Christian Church (Disciples of Christ): An Interpretative Examination in the Cultural Context*. Bethany Press, 1973 (out of print).

Boring, M. Eugene, *Disciples and the Bible: A History of Disciples Biblical Interpretation in North America*. Chalice Press, 1997.

Cartwright, Colbert S., *Candles of Grace: Disciples Worship in Perspective*. Chalice Press, 1992.

——. *People of the Chalice: Disciples of Christ in Faith and Practice*. Chalice Press, 1988. Study guide by Colbert Cartwright.

Cummins, D. Duane, *A Handbook for Today's Disciples*, revised. Christian Board of Publication, 1991.

Dixon, Michael E., editor, *Prepare the Way for Baptism and Membership*. Christian Board of Publication, 1998.

Dunnavant, Anthony L., editor, *Cane Ridge in Context: Perspectives on Barton W. Stone and the Revival*. Disciples of Christ Historical Society, 1992.

Friedly, Robert L., and D. Duane Cummins, *The Search for Identity: Disciples of Christ—The Restructure Years*. Chalice Press, 1987.

Fuqua, Vicky, *Heritage Trek: A Walk Through Disciples History*, a resource for grades 5-8. Christian Board of Publication, 1996.

Garrett, Leroy, *The Stone Campbell Movement*. College Press, 1994.

Gonzalez, Justo L., *Manana: Christian Theology from a Hispanic Perspective*. Abingdon Press, 1990.

Hamm, Richard L., *From Mainline to Front Line*. Lexington Theological Quarterly, 1996.

Hull, Debra, *Christian Church Women: Shapers of a Movement*. Chalice Press, 1994.

Lawrence, Kenneth, ed., *Classic Themes of Disciples Theology*. Texas Christian University Press, 1986.

McAllister, Lester G., *An Alexander Campbell Reader*. Chalice Press, 1988.

Mead, Frank S., revised by Samuel S. Hill, *Handbook of Denominations in the United States New Tenth Edition*. Abingdon, 1995.

Osborn, Ronald E., *The Faith We Affirm*. Christian Board of Publication, 1979.

Paulsell, William O., *Disciples at Prayer: The Spirituality of the Christian Church (Disciples of Christ)*. Chalice Press and Disciples of Christ Historical Society, 1995.

Randall, Eugene, *From the Balcony to the Boardroom: A Brief History of Black Disciples in Kentucky and Surrounding Regions*. Amspeedy.

Richesin, L. Dale, and Larry D. Bouchard, eds. *Interpreting Disciples: Practical Theology in the Disciples of Christ*. Texas Christian University Press, 1987.

Sprinkle, Stephen V., *Disciples and Theology: Understanding the Faith of a People in Covenant*. Chalice Press, 1997.

Stemmler, Guin, *A Mini-History of the Christian Church (Disciples of Christ)*, second revision. Christian Board of Publication, 1996.

Toulouse, Mark G., *Joined in Discipleship: The Shaping of Contemporary Disciples Identity*, rev. ed. Chalice Press, 1997.

Tucker, William E., and Lester G. McAllister, *Journey in Faith*. Chalice Press, 1975.

Watkins, Keith, editor, *Baptism and Belonging*. Chalice Press, 1991. Study guide by William Rose-Heim.

——. *Thankful Praise: A Resource for Christian Worship*. Chalice Press, 1987. Study guide by J. Cy Rowell.

Williams, D. Newell, editor, *A Case Study of Mainstream Protestantism: The Disciples' Relation to American Culture, 1880–1989*. William Eerdmans/Chalice Press, 1991.

The Nature of the Church Series, published by Christian Board of Publication for the Council on Christian Unity, examines the Commission on Theology reports:

- *What Sort of Church Are We?* by James O. Duke.
- *What Is Our Authority?* by William Baird, 1983.
- *Ministry Among Disciples: Past, Present, and Future* by D. Newell Williams, 1985.
- *Baptism: Embodiment of the Gospel* by Clark Williamson, 1987.
- *The Lord's Supper* by James O. Duke and Richard L. Harrison, Jr., 1993.

Disciples Thumbnail Sketches (series of brochures) cover topics of:

- Baptism
- Characteristic Beliefs of the Christian Church
- The Church at Worship
- The Lord's Supper
- The Meaning of Church Membership
- Our Church, Our History